JOURNAL OF ERITREAN STUDIES

EDITOR
YONAS MESFUN ASFAHA
College of Education (CoE)

I0589670

EDITORIAL STAFF

ISSA ADEM
Col. of Busi. & Soc. Sciences (CBSS)
RAHEL ASGHEDOM
Writer

SALEH MAHMUD
CoE
SENAI WOLDEAB
CBSS

EDITORIAL BOARD

ALEMSEGED TESFAY
Res. & Doc. Center
ALESSANDRO BAUSI
Universität Hamburg
ALESSANDRO VOLTERRA
Università Roma Tre
ASGHEDE HAGOS
Delaware State University
ASMEROM KIDANE
University of Dar es Salaam
BAIRU TAFLA
Universität Hamburg
CHRISTINE MATZKE
Bayreuth University
GEBRE HIWET TESFAGIORGIS
Iowa State University
GEORGIA COLE
The University of Edinburgh
GIANFRANCESCO LUSINI
Università di Napoli "L'Orientale"

RAINER VOIGT
Freie Universität Berlin
SENAIT BAHTA
CBSS
SJAAK KROON
Tilburg University
TEJ N. DHAR
CBSS
TESFAY ARADOM
Roxbury Comm. College
TESFAY TEWOLDE
Florence University
WOLDETENSAE TEWOLDE
CBSS
YACOB FISSEHA (Emeritus)
Michigan State University
ZACCARIA MASSIMO
Università di Pavia
ZEMENFES TSIGHE
Nat. Hig. Edu. & Res. Inst.

ADVISORY BOARD

ABBEBE KIFLEYESUS
CBSS
ASMAROM LEGESSE (Emeritus)
Citizens for Peace
CHARLES CANTALUPO
Pennsylvania State University

GEBRENEGUS GHILAGABER
Stockholm University
IQBAL D. JHAZBHAY
UNISA
RICH ROSEN (Emeritus)
UNC (Chapel Hill)

CONTENTS

INTRODUCTION

Woldetnsae Tewolde
Introduction

ARTICLES

Abiel Y. Weldegiorgis and Zemenfes Tsighe
Monitoring Land Use/Land Cover Change Using Satellite Images, GIS
and Spatial Metrics in Keren sub-Zone, Eritrea...1

Elias Gebreluul and Zekeria Abdelkerim
Distribution of Mangrove Forest along the Eritrean Red Sea Coast
Using Sentinel-2 Data (2017)...35

Hadgu Eyesab Kidanemariam, Zekeria Abdelkerim and Habtom Emru Hagos
Seasonal correlation of changes on SST and Surface Chl-*a* in the
Southern Red Sea: based on remote sensing...55

Hammid Mohammed Ibrahim and Md. Minhajul Hoda
A Geospatial Approach to Malaria Risk Analysis in Ne'us Zoba
Ghindae, Eritrea...75

Mebrahtom Zerom and Ogbaghebriel Berakhi
Assessment of Land Degradation Vulnerability through Land Use/Land
Cover Change Detection in Tsmieti Catchment, Ne'us Zoba Adi
Kuala...105

Mohammed Mohammedali Mussa and Woldeselassie Ogbazghi
Land Use-Land Cover Change Detection Using Remote Sensing data
and Geographical Information System (GIS) Tools in Arid Lowlands of
Eritrea...135

Tsinat Yemane and Zemenfes Tsighe
Evaluation of Accessibility to Primary, Middle and Secondary Schools:
Case Study of Adi QeyyiH sub-Zone, Eritrea...155

A note from the editorial team

The editorial team of the Journal of Eritrean Studies acknowledges the long delay between the publications of this issue and the previous issue. The delay is mainly attributed to the national steps taken in Eritrea in relation to the COVID-19 pandemic and some other administrative inconveniences. We will work hard to continue to publish this journal at regular intervals.

This issue has seven articles. It starts with a study of land use and land cover changes observed in the sub-Zone of Keren in Anseba region. Using satellite images, GIS and spatial metrics, Abiel Y. Weldegiorgis and Zemenfes Tsighe have found that built-up area has grown almost 500 percent in the last three decades leading to the year 2015. Elias Gebreluul and Zekeria Abdelkerim, using remote sensing data, studied the distribution of mangrove forest along the Red Sea coast. Hadgu Eyesab, Zekeria Abdelkerim and Habtom Emru's study investigated seasonal and spatial relationship of sea surface temperature (SST) and surface chlorophyll-a (Chl-*a*) concentration and SST and nutrient availability in southern Red Sea using satellite data. Hammid Mohammed Ibrahim and Md. Minhajul Hoda's study used geospatial approach to malaria risk analysis in Ghindae sub-Zone. The study by Mebrahtom Zerom and Ogbaghebriel Berakhi assessed land degradation in Tsmieti catchment, Adi Kuala sub-Zone, using land use/land cover change analysis through landsat images taken at three points in time (1994, 2002, and 2015). Mohammed Mohammedali Mussa and Woldeselassie Ogbazghi's study used satellite remote sensing and GIS to monitor land use/land cover changes in Hamelmalo sub-Zone. Finally, Tsinat Yemane and Zemenfes Tsighe assessed accessibility to primary, middle and secondary schools in Adi QeyyiH sub-Zone using GIS.

Special Issue: Studies on Geo-informatics and Remote Sensing in Eritrea

Introductory Note

Woldetnsae Tewolde[1]

The articles presented in this special issue of the Journal of Eritrean Studies are the outcomes of a postgraduate program that run between 2015 and 2018 at the former College of Arts and Social Sciences before it was replaced, as the result of restructuring of the institutions of higher education, by the College of Business and Social Sciences in 2018. The postgraduate program (M.Sc.) in Geo-informatics at the then College of Arts and Social Sciences (CASS) was made possible in collaboration with University of Helsinki (UH), Finland, and the relentless efforts made by key government institutions in the country. The program had the following objectives: (a) to develop the students' problem solving skills and enhances scientific understanding of issues related to spatial information; (b) to produce qualified candidates that would ultimately teach undergraduate students the principles and skills of Geo-informatics at the institutes of higher learning; and (c) to meet the demand for highly qualified personnel in the various public institutions of Eritrea.

At the beginning, preliminary needs assessment was conducted to get critical insight into the interests and needs towards the proposed academic program and to evaluate the demand for skilled manpower. The assessment enabled to identify the extent to which the program could be applied in teaching and researching. During start-up of the program, CASS enjoyed a wide range of support from various government institutions with the

[1] Associate Dean for Academic Affairs, College of Business and Social Sciences, Eritrea. Email: wolde1956@gmail.com.

following two notable examples. Firstly, comments and feedback obtained from Eritrea Mapping and Information Center were instrumental in bringing the curriculum to its final shape. Secondly, the process of procuring equipment for the state-of-the-art geographic information system (GIS) lab was made possible as a result of cooperation from the Red Sea Trading Corporation. The project was funded by development cooperation funds from the Ministry for Foreign Affairs of Finland. The Finnish National Agency for Education, the National Higher Education and Research Institute of Eritrea, and experts from UH (Prof. Petri Pellikka and Mr. Pekka Hurskainen) and CASS had all contributed towards the success of the project.

The graduates of the M.Sc. program are now equipped with knowledge at advanced level to solve complex geographical problems in terms of theory, methodology and empiricism. The breadth and interdisciplinary nature of the program was expected to enable graduates to deal with tasks and projects related to sustainable use of resources. The graduates of the program have since been engaged in teaching at Eritrean colleges and have continued to engage in research. An indicator of the admirable level of the quality of education they were exposed to in the program is this special issue of the Journal of Eritrean Studies dedicated to publishing seven peer-reviewed articles extracted from the theses they submitted – some with the co-authorship of senior colleagues – as part of the postgraduate program.

Monitoring Land Use/Land Cover Change Using Satellite Images, GIS and Spatial Metrics in Keren sub-Zone, Eritrea

Abiel Y. Weldegiorgis[1] and Zemenfes Tsighe[2]

Abstract

Urban growth patterns and the subsequent consumption of agricultural areas on the peri-urban areas is among the most prominent forms of land use and land cover change in most urban areas and the surrounding fringes. They are particularly prominent in most major Eritrean towns, such as Keren, where the structure and size of the traditional city has undergone significant changes. A systematic analysis and description of the land use and land cover change induced by rapid urbanization within the urban and peri-urban landscape is essential for detection of environmental changes and their related causes. Therefore, land use and land cover change was quantified for the last 31 years within and in the vicinity of Keren, which is one of the fast-growing towns in Eritrea, using Landsat images, geographic information systems (GIS), and spatial metrics. In order to achieve this, satellite data of Landsat TM for 1984 and 1994; ETM+ for 2002 and OLI-TIRS for 2015 were obtained and preprocessed using GRASS GIS 7.0.5. Then, the land use and land cover maps were generated using a pixel-based image classification approach with the application of Maximum Likelihood algorithm in QGIS2.18 using the SCP plugin. Classification was assessed using the overall accuracy and Kappa measure of agreement. These measures of accuracies are found to be above the minimum standard acceptable level. The land use dynamics, both for pattern and quantities, were also studied using a post classification change detection technique together with selected spatial/landscape metrics; namely class area, number of patches, edge density, largest patch index, Euclidian mean nearest neighbor distance, area weighted mean patch fractal dimension,

---

[1] Lecturer, College of Business and Social Sciences, Eritrea. Email: yohannesabiel5@gmail.com.
[2] Director, Bureau of Higher Education Administration and International Linkages, National Higher Education and Research Institute, Eritrea. Email: zemenfest@gmail.com.

contagion and clumpy. Results indicated that the built-up area has grown by 473 percent between 1984 and 2015 while valuable land cover/land use classes like agricultural areas suffered severe losses. Analysis of the spatial metrics has also revealed that the town has shown significant signs of sprawling evidenced by higher degree of fragmentation of the developments. Since such works are not widely practiced yet in Eritrea, the land use maps produced in this study will contribute to both the development of sustainable urban land use planning decisions and also for forecasting possible future changes in growth patterns.

Keywords: land use and land cover; spatial metrics; accuracy assessment; Keren sub-Zone; Eritrea.

1. Introduction

Due to rapid expansion of urbanization, large tracts of rural land have been converted into urban space. From the land use and land cover change point of view, such expansion is of greater importance because of its strong effect on other land cover classes, such as agricultural lands, non-built-up areas, forests and others. Human induced land use and land cover change is the most important component of global environmental change with impacts possibly greater than the other global changes (Turner, Meyer and Skole, 1994; Jensen, 2005; Jensen, Gatrel, and Mclean, 2007; Lumbin *et al.*, 2001). Like other anthropogenic-environment interactions, urban land cover changes respond to socioeconomic, political, cultural, demographic and environmental conditions, largely characterized by a concentration of humans (Masek, Lindsay and Goward, 2000).

In spite of their small area coverage relative to the earth's surface, dynamic urban growth processes, particularly the expansion of urban population in a larger extent and urbanized area, have a significant impact on natural and human environment at all geographic scales (Herold, Couclelis, and Clarke, 2005).

Consequently, the issue of land use changes has been considered in many international and interdisciplinary researches such as remote sensing, political ecology, and biogeography (Turner, Meyer, and Skole, 1994; Jensen, 2005). Moreover, since the 1990s, global, regional, and local studies of land use and land cover have greatly increased due to advances in observation and detection methods including remote sensing and related techniques. Hence, studies in land use and land cover change of urban areas will play an important role in monitoring urban land use changes and ensure sustainable urban development.

Even though urban land use changes have been studied for many years, the advent of satellite images and geospatial technologies has opened new dimensions for assessing and monitoring land use and land cover change. As frequently stated in the literature, because of their cost effectiveness and temporal frequency, remote sensing approaches are widely used for the detection and analysis of changes (Im and Tullis, 2008; Brink *et al.*, 2014), examining the development of urban sprawl (Araya and Hergaten, 2008; Araya and Cabral, 2010; Tewolde and Cabral, 2011), quantifying urban growth and land use dynamics (Herold, Goldstain, and Clarke, 2003), landscape pattern analysis (Li and Yeh, 2004), and urbanization (Weng, 2007).

Eritrea, with 22 percent of the entire population residing in urban places, had the sixth highest urban population growth rate in Eastern Africa for the years 2010 - 2015, where the annual urban population growth was 1.9% (Abiel Y., 2018, p. 188). In spite of its low urbanization level compared to other African countries, the impact of land use and land cover change has become a big challenge to the country. Keren sub-Zone, where this study was conducted, has also experienced great changes. The environmental conditions of Keren were relatively healthy, endowed with fertile agricultural area in the plains for rain fed and irrigated agricultural activities, scenic beauty and lower pollution.

3

However, nowadays, the scenario has been comparatively reversed as the resources and environmental condition are being degraded due to rapid urbanization. Therefore, there is an immediate need for proper land use and land cover studies of the sub-Zone valuing the land resources for economic and environmental sustainability.

Although Eritrean land use systems have attracted research interests over the last decades, the complexity of land use change processes has been less in focus. A thorough insight into the land use change processes has accordingly been difficult to establish, not least due to the lack of reliable, site specific information not only on land use, but also on key driving forces of land use change. Emphasizing situation-specific interactions among a large number of factors at different spatial and temporal scales, thus, became a key issue in the interdisciplinary research program of Geoinformatics Eritrea (GIERI), of which this research has been part. This research work, thus, aims at providing novel perspectives to the understanding of land change processes in Keren sub-Zone with a special emphasis to the patterns of urban changes. Moreover, it aims at providing quantitative and spatial information on developments of the urban space in the study area using an integrated approach of GIS, remote sensing and spatial metrics.

2. Objective of the study

The major aim of this paper is to detect, quantify, and analyze land use and land cover change in general and urban land use changes in particular in Keren sub-Zone using remotely sensed data. In order to attain the major aim, the following specific objectives are specified in sequence to:

- Generate land use and land cover maps of Keren sub-Zone for the years 1984, 1994, 2002 and 2015;

- Evaluate the accuracy assessment of the classification techniques used;
- Make a thorough assessment of land use and land cover during the four temporal time spans of the study time periods, i.e. 1984 to 1994, 1994 to 2002, 2002 to 2015, and 1984 to 2015;
- Analyze the land use and land cover transitions of the land classes and identify the gains and losses of the land classes in relation to built-up areas; and
- Identify and characterize the impacts of urban land use change on other land classes.

3. Study area

The study area is Keren sub-Zone, one of the eight sub-Zones of the Anseba administrative region. Keren is located in the central high land of Eritrea covering a total area of about 9,899 hectares. This is Eritrea's second largest town. In relative terms, Keren is found 91 kms North West of the capital city of Eritrea, Asmara, along the road to Tesseney. The geographical extension of the sub-Zone Keren is 15°43'50"N to 15°50'20"N and 38°20'40"E to 38°29'40E, with an elevation ranging from 1324 mts. to 1896 mts. above sea level. Geographically, the study area is characterized by extensive and narrow plateau of undulating landscape. It is interrupted by mountain ranges and incise driver valleys. The study area is highly vulnerable to land degradation.

Keren has been one of the fastest growing urban areas in the country during the last three decades of independence. This has resulted in an uncontrolled urban sprawl with negative consequences such as loss of agricultural land, destruction of vegetation cover, air pollution, housing scarcity, overcrowding, encroachment, slums, unregulated disposal of waste, increasing water scarcity and pollution (DUD, 2005; MLWE, 2012; MoA, 2002). Due to its geographical nature, i.e., the limits set by the mountains to the South (Mt Ziban and Mt. Et'abir), East (Mt.

Senkil), North West (Mt. Lalimba) and North East (Mt. Bambi) land is a scarce resource in Keren sub-Zone. Hence, the town sprawls along a narrow basin surrounded by these granitic mountains on all sides. The town is under a great pressure due to the rapid urban expansion. Nevertheless, built-up areas have tended to ignore the topography, hydrograph, natural site as well as fertile land.

Rapid development, economic growth, and increasing employment opportunities in Keren have attracted people from all over the country in general and the administrative zone in particular, increasing the city's population to around 91,271 in 2017 according to reports of the statistics office of the sub-Zone. The land under agriculture within the city's boundaries has decreased with both legal and illegal development, while migration of people from rural areas in search of employment and better wages continues to stress public services. Moreover, efforts by the Government of Eritrea in 1996 to establish Keren as an administrative seat of Anseba zone led to several changes in policies on the development of infrastructure and facilities, as well as in relevant public sectors.

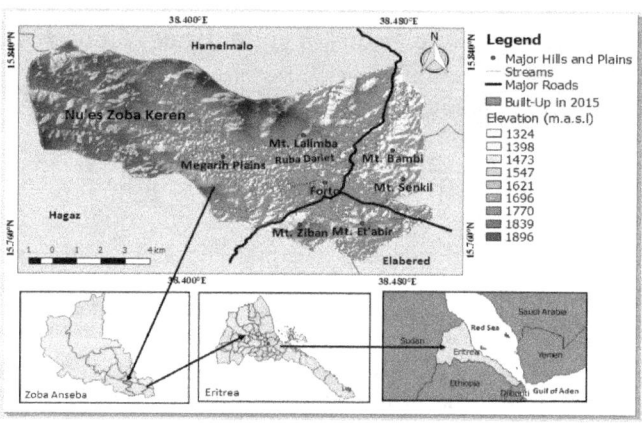

Figure 1. Locational map of the study area.

4. Data

This study used a suit of Landsat images collected from the U.S. Geological Survey (USGS) to assess the urbanization effects of Keren's expansion and sprawling trend, including two Landsat TM images acquired on 28 October 1984, 22 September 1994, one ETM+ acquired on 20 September 2002, and one Landsat OLI-TIRS image acquired on 2 October 2015. Data was projected to a World Geodetic System (WGS) 1984, Universal Transverse Mercator (UTM), Zone_37N coordinate system. A 30m spatial resolution Digital Elevation Model (DEM) was also downloaded from SRTM DEM. Data on main roads and main rivers were obtained from the GIS and Statistics Office of Anseba zone. High resolution imageries were also obtained from the Ministry of Land, Water and Environment, Department of Land, and Eritrean Mapping and Information Center of the President's Office. These are SPOT-5, with 5mts. spatial resolution acquired in 2006 and IKONOS, with 2 mts. spatial resolution acquired in 2001. Google Earth (time slide) was also used for preliminary interpretation of the historical imageries of the sub-Zone. All of these ancillary data have been used during sample collection for image classification and accuracy assessment.

5. Methods

A. Image pre-processing

The Landsat TM, ETM+ and Landsat OLI-TIRS data were geometrically and radiometrically corrected to account for positional errors and atmospheric inferences (Masek, Lindsay, and Goward, 2000). Though some basic processing has already been done by the USGS, further image pre-processing and preparation was performed in GRASS GIS 7.0.5 to further topographically correct the image so as to effectively reduce the shadows in the satellite images which is primarily caused by variation in illumination due to varying topography. Such phenomenon usually happens when the observed target area contains hilly or mountainous regions, where the slopes cause variations in the brightness reflectance (terrain effects), which can lead to wrong classification results (Neteler *et al.*, 2012). To overcome this problem, a terrain correction (illumination correction) based on the local slopes derived from an elevation model has been applied (Figure 2). Therefore, since the built-up areas in Keren sub-Zone are surrounded by mountains conducting a topographic correction was deemed necessary. This was done by modeling the illumination conditions when the satellite image was taken. To do so, first an illumination model was calculated using terrain aspect and slope angles derived from the DEM of SRTM with 30 mts. spatial resolution, and solar zenith and azimuth angles derived from the Landsat metadata as input variables. Following this, another model of Terrain-corrected reflectance was calculated for each Landsat band utilizing the illumination model and the c-factor correction method provided by GRASS GIS.

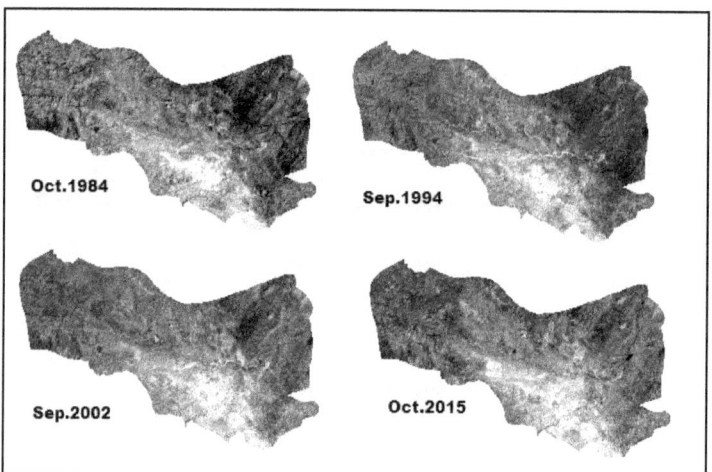

Figure 2. Topographically corrected and enhanced Landsat images of Keren sub-Zone.

Abiel Y. Weldegiorgis and Zemenfes Tsighe

B. Classification schemes

The land use and land cover classes applied in this paper are adopted from Global Cover land use and land cover classification scheme produced in 2009. For the sake of simplicity, the researchers modified the descriptions of some of the land use and land cover classes considering the land use/land cover of the study area.

No	LULC Classes	Simplified Description on the basis of Global Cover (2009)
1	Built-Up	Industrial, commercial, public built ups; and urban green areas transportation and other continuous and non-continuous urban fabrics and related built up areas
2	Agricultural	Arable land including rain fed and irrigated fields, fallowed fields, Permanent crops, and Heterogeneous agricultural areas
3	Grassland and Shrubs	Grazing areas, grass land, and shrubs
4	Bare Land	All vacant spaces, rocky areas, cleared lands
5	Intermittent Streams	Seasonally flowing streams, and sand marches
6	Water Body	Water reservoirs like dams and ponds

Table 1. Description of land use and land cover classes.
Source: modified from Global Cover classification scheme, 2009.

C. Pixel based image classification using the SCP plugin of QGIS

There are two primary types of pixel-based classification algorithms applied to remotely sensed data: unsupervised and supervised. Unsupervised classification algorithms cluster data according to several user-defined statistical parameters in an iterative fashion until either some percentage of pixels remain unchanged or a maximum number of iterations have been performed (Cohen and Goward, 2004). This method of classification is most useful when no previous knowledge or ground truth data of an area is available.

However, the classes determined by the algorithm still require land cover identification by an experienced analyst, which can be a significant disadvantage in using this method. In supervised classification, the image analyst supervises the pixel categorization process (Neteler *et al.*, 2012; Yang *et al.*, 2003; Weng, 2012; Im, Jensen and Tullis, 2008; Benz *et al.*, 2004).

In this project the supervised classification method was applied for the land use and land cover classification with QGIS2.18 using semi-automatic plugin (SCP). Subsequently land cover maps were generated based on the pixel using supervised classification through a number of processes (Figure 3). The first step was collection of training samples for each land cover class which are typically representative of land cover classes. These samples were collected based on the researchers' field and physiographical observations of the study area.

Moreover, image enhancement and composition were applied for better determination of land cover classes. Seed algorithm (region growing) and polygon drawing approaches were used to train the region of interest (ROI). Using these approaches training samples were collected for each of the Landsat imageries. In this stage, a number of both classification and reclassification procedures were used in order to improve the classification and neglect misclassified cells. Further classification refinements were performed by reassigning scattered pixels and merging of small pixels inside bigger class. These were only for image objects less than four pixels in size using the sieve module under raster tool in QGIS. Otherwise, no smoothing and generalization of pixels were done, in order not to influence the change detection and modeling

Abiel Y. Weldegiorgis and Zemenfes Tsighe

processes (Tewolde, 2011). The 1984, 1994, 2002 and 2015 images were hence classified into six classes. The overall total area of the land use classes of the study area was 9899.28 hectare.

D. Accuracy assessment

The classification accuracy assessments of the resulting land use and land cover layers of satellite images were carried out by comparing the sample land use and land cover class of the classified layer and the reference layer. In this study, a total number of 350 test samples for all four images were randomly generated from the original mosaic image of 1984. Examination of the test sample plots was done and they were referenced and labeled a class value for each image by comparing them against Google earth image of the specific year for the images of 1984, 1994, and 2002 (due to lack of high resolution satellite data) and also high resolution IKONOS image of 2001 was also used for the 2002 classified image. The accuracy assessment was conducted for each classification result.

However, different sampling procedures and techniques were used to assess the accuracy of the 2015 image. During the field visit, the researchers collected reference data sets using GNSS as a way points and produced 786 random points. For these waypoints to be applicable and used in the SCP (Semi-Automatic Classification) plugin of the QGIS it has to be in either raster file format or vector polygon. This problem was solved by creating a 5m buffer around the points and creating polygons.

These field generated points were later to be integrated with the 350 randomly generated points. Since some parts of the sub-Zone were inaccessible because of the rugged topography and fear of landmines, integration of these randomly generated and later referenced using the Google earth image points was deemed necessary to complement the scarcity of reference points in some

11

areas of the study site which were not covered by the GNSS reading.

Hence a total of 1,136 test samples were used for image classification and validation of 2015. Out of the 1,136 points 70%, i.e. 795 points, were used for classification and the rest 30%, i.e. 341 points, were used for validation or accuracy assessment. The selection of these points was performed using systematic sampling procedure.

E. Analysis of past land use/land cover change

In this study, post-classification change detection technique was used to characterize land use and land cover dynamics in Keren sub-Zone between 1984 and 2015. The method chosen depends on the nature of the study and the type of imagery available. Based on the scope of this study, the PCC method was preferred, which has been broadly accepted in RS to identify change among multi-temporal data (Jacob *et al.*, 2017; Minta *et al.*, 2018; Hayes and Cohen, 2007; Shalaby and Tateishi, 2007; Im, Jensen, and Tullis, 2008; Zhu, Woodcock, and Olofsson, 2012; Lu *et al.*, 2004).

In this section, land use and land cover changes are investigated in four temporal periods: 1984-1994, 1994-2002, 2002-2015 and 1984-2015. As mentioned above, the images for the years 1984, 1994, 2002 and 2015 were classified independently. However, the classification algorithm developed for each of the four images was the same and the samples collected were also similar. Therefore, the problem of inconsistency is believed to be less, and hence the accuracy level of the post classification remains the same like the classified images.

In this study, two different and somehow complementary approaches have also been used to describe the changes that occurred in Keren in the past three decades: CROSSTAB and

Land Change Modeler (LCM) functions from TerrSet Geospatial Monitoring and Modeling System, of the Idrisi Software.

F. Calculation of spatial metrics

In this study, the changes in urban landscape (e.g., development of discontinuous urban areas or urban fragmentation) are measured and analyzed at a class level using the FRAGSTATS software, version 4.2.1. A number of metrics have been developed to describe and quantify elements of patch shape complexity and spatial configuration relative to other patch types (Ji *et al.*, 2006).

From the numerous metrics developed so far, it is not clear which will prove to be the most informative and interpretable over large areas and hence it leads to the application of various metrics of different types in a similar and related studies.

In this study eight spatial metrics, which have already been used in various publications, were adopted and used for analyzing the built-up land cover changes. These spatial metrics are: Total Area (CA/TA), Number of Patches (NP), Edge Density (ED), Area Weighted Mean Patch Fractal Dimension (FRAC_AM), Largest Patch Index (LPI), Euclidean Mean Nearest Neighbor (ENN_MN), Contagion (CONTAG), and Clumpiness Index (CLUMPY). The selection of the metrics was based on their applications in previous research works on urban areas (Araya and Cabral, 2010; Herold, Goldstain and Clarke, 2003; Megahed *et al.*, 2015; Padmanaban *et al.*, 2017).

Metrics	Description	Units	Range
CA–Class Area	The sum of the areas of all urban patches, that is, the total urban area in the landscape.	Hectares	CA > 0, no limit
NP–Number of Patches	The number of urban patches in the landscape.	None	NP ≥ 1, no limit
ED–Edge Density	The sum of the lengths of all edge segments involving the urban patch type, divided by the total landscape area.	Mts./ m²	ED ≥ 0, no limit
LPI–Largest Patch Index	Area of the largest patch of the corresponding patch types divided by total area covered by urban.	%	0 < LPI ≤ 100
ENN_MN–Euclidian mean nearest neighbor distance	The distance mean value over all urban patches to the nearest neighboring urban patch, based on shortest edge-to-edge distance from cell center to cell center.	Mts.	ENN_MN > 0, no limit
FRAC_AM–Area Weighted Mean Patch Fractal Dimension	Area weighted mean value of the fractal dimension values of all urban patches, the fractal dimension of a patch equals two times the logarithm of patch perimeter divided by the logarithm of patch area; the perimeter is adjusted to correct for the raster bias in perimeter.	None	1 ≤ AWMPFD ≤ 2
CONTAG–Contagion	Measures the overall probability that a cell of a patch type is adjacent to cells of the same type.	%	0 < CONTAG ≤ 100
CLUMPY – Clumpiness Index	Measure the clumpiness of patches in urban areas.	None	-1 ≤CLUMPY≤1

Table 2. Spatial metrics adopted and used in the study.

6. Results and discussions

A. Land cover classification and accuracy assessment

The classification results for 1984, 1994, 2002, and 2015 were assessed using randomly extracted points from the ground and high-resolution images reference data. The comparison results between these two datasets (i.e., classification pixels and ground reference pixels) indicated that the values of the overall accuracy obtained for 1984, 1994, 2002, and 2015 were 85.43%, 85.71%, 86.57% and 87.39%, respectively (Table 3). The Kappa coefficient measuring the agreement between the classification and ground reference maps with a value of 1 and 0 respectively representing perfect agreement and no agreement indicated the satisfactory agreement between the two datasets. The Kappa coefficient values obtained for 1984, 1994, 2002, and 2015 were 0.81, 0.82, 0.83, and 0.84, respectively (Table 3).

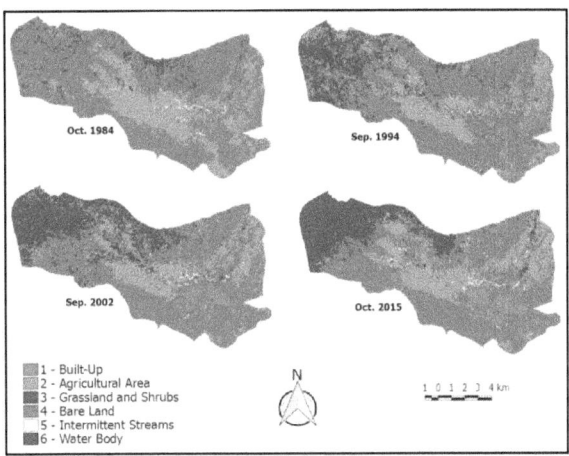

Figure 3. Land-Cover map of the study area.

The areal proportion of each land use and land cover classes of the study area under the study years is graphically provided as follows (Figure 4 and Table 4).

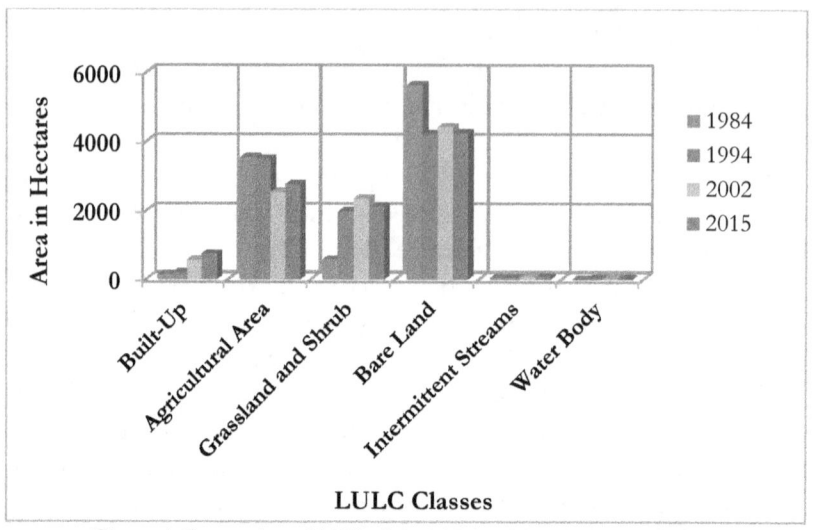

Figure 4. Proportion of LULC in 1984, 1994, 2002, and 2015.

Class Name	1984		1994		2002		2015	
	Produ cer's	Use r's	Produ cer's	Use r's	Produ cer's	Use r's	Produ cer's	Use r's
Built-Up	89.71%	88.41%	92.06%	85.29%	91.80%	94.92%	96.86%	90.59%
Agricultural Land	85.11%	88.89%	87.10%	88.04%	86.02%	89.89%	86.51%	84.50%
Grassland &Shrubs	81.67%	83.05%	83.08%	88.52%	89.66%	85.25%	88.64%	93.98%
Bare Land	86.73%	90.43%	85.86%	88.54%	85.19%	88.46%	84.66%	91.39%
Intermittent Streams	86.36%	61.29%	66.67%	52.63%	68.42%	50%	54.55%	51.43%
Water Body	62.50%	71.43%	80%	85.71%	90.91%	90.91%	88.24%	83.33%
Over-All	85.43%		85.71%		86.57%		87.37%	
Kappa	0.81		0.82		0.83		0.84	

Table 3. Validation of land use and land cover classes.

B. Land use and land cover dynamics (1984-2015)

Landscapes of the study site have experienced a marked change in land use and land cover over the last three decades (Tables 4 and 5; Fig. 5). In 1984, the landscape was dominated principally by bare land and agricultural area that covered 57% and 36% respectively of the total area (4203, and 3487 ha respectively). However, analysis of four-time periods (1984, 1994, 2002 and 2015) revealed progressive expansion of grassland and shrubs between 1984 and 2002 in which it grew by about 249% from 1984 to 1994, and has become among dominant land use types since early 1990s (Figure 4 and 5).

Currently, more than two third (70.52%) of the total area is under agricultural area and bare land, while grassland and shrubs, and built-up area occupy only 21% and 7% respectively. Over the entire study period, the coverage of built-up area, grassland and shrubs, water body and intermittent streams increased by 473%, 274%, 187% and 51%, respectively, while bare land, and agricultural area declined by 25% and 22%, respectively (Table 5).

The rate and trend of changes varied markedly between land uses, and intervals of the study period. Built-Up area expanded slowly between 1984 and 1994, at a rate of 4.5% per annum. However, accelerated expansion, at a rate of 25% per annum, occurred between 1994 and 2002. Since mid-2000's built-up area did not change appreciably. Unlike periods before 2002, a declining growth in built-Up area was seen at a minimal rate of 3% per annum between 2002 and 2015. This is largely attributed to the nationwide moratorium imposed on private construction sector after 2005. Grassland and shrubs, which occupied only 5.7% (565 ha) in 1984, has shown a dramatic increase, in which it exceptionally expanded at a rate of 25% per annum between 1984 and 1994, and reached 21 % (2115 ha) of the total area in 2015. This is mainly attributed to the fact that the first image was taken in 1984, during the severe five drought years of 1982 to 1986, however the remaining images of the years 1994, 2002 and 2015 were taken during a much improved conditions of the vegetation.

Moreover, since the region is among the places that witnessed some of the great battles of the Second World War and war for independence, the presence of landmines which are still waiting to be cleared off of the area may have further contributed for the rapid regeneration of the vegetation of the area. The field visit also supports the claim made by Boerma (2012) that factors like war, fear of the Ethiopian military and the proliferation of land mines resulted in limited use of distant pasture which further contributed to the regeneration of woodlands because of the increased inaccessibility of certain areas due to risks posed by landmines.

Water body increased substantially with rates higher than intermittent streams, bare land and agricultural area land use and land cover type in the same time periods (Table 5). It expanded at a rate of 18.7% per annum in periods between 1984 and 2015. Intermittent streams which meagerly flowed and covered only 0.41% of the total area in 1984 also increased by 51% between 1984 and 2015 at a rate of 1.65% per annum (Table 5). The dynamics in the intermittent streams was irregular, and might be attributed to highly erratic and unpredictable regimes of the annual rainfall in the study area. Accelerated expansion at a rate of 4.6% per annum occurred between 1994 and 2002.

Nevertheless, the results and interpretations for the intermittent streams needs to be taken with caution for it has a lower classification accuracy from all other land cover classes, and hence the changes could be either due to actual change or errors in classification. Moreover, the limitations from the quality of remote sensing data, especially coarse resolutions (30 m × 30 m pixel size) of satellite images, can affect the precision to describe small size features like very narrow streams and it is expected that there is high probability of generalization.

Agricultural area which falls under a variety of tenure system and access also experienced a remarkable decline over the last 31 years. Between 1984 and 1994, conversion of agricultural area to other uses was slow at a rate of 0.14% per annum. However, 28% of the total area under agricultural area in 1984 was converted into other land uses between 1994 and 2002 at an alarming rate of 3.4% per annum. The rate of conversion, however, decreased to 0.62% between 2002 and 2015 (Table 5).

Recent minimal rate of conversion and position of most areas on landscapes most vulnerable to seasonal water logging may suggest the exhaustion of suitable land under agricultural area for other uses. A drastic decline in agricultural area may also suggest that sustained increase in food production in the sub-Zone was not based on the availability of cultivable lands.

However, bare land was the most dominant land use and land cover class on the landscape during the study time. That particular land cover class was reduced from 57% to 43% in periods between 1984 and 2015. The highest rate of decline took place during the first temporal spans, 1984 –1994, at the rate of 2.5% per annum. This is greatly attributed to the fact that much of the contribution to the rapid expansion of the grass land and shrubs within this temporal time span was made from bare land.

		1984		1994		2002		2015	
1	Built-Up	127.6	1.29 %	184.6	1.86 %	548.2	5.54 %	731.6	7.39%
2	Agricultural Area	3535.8	35.72 %	3486.6	35.22 %	2540.4	25.66 %	2746.4	27.74 %
3	Grassland and Shrub	565.2	5.71 %	1969.8	19.90 %	2340.8	23.65 %	2115.1	21.37 %
4	Bare Land	5626.7	56.84 %	4202.7	42.45 %	4403.0	44.48 %	4235.0	42.78 %
5	Intermitten t Streams	40.3	0.41 %	39.6	0.40 %	54.4	0.55 %	60.9	0.62%
6	Water Body	3.6	0.04 %	15.9	0.16 %	12.5	0.13 %	10.4	0.10%
	Category Total	9899.3	100%	9899.3	100%	9899.3	100%	9899.3	100%

Table 4. Area in hectare and percentage of LULC classes for 1984, 1994, 2002, and 2015 in Keren.

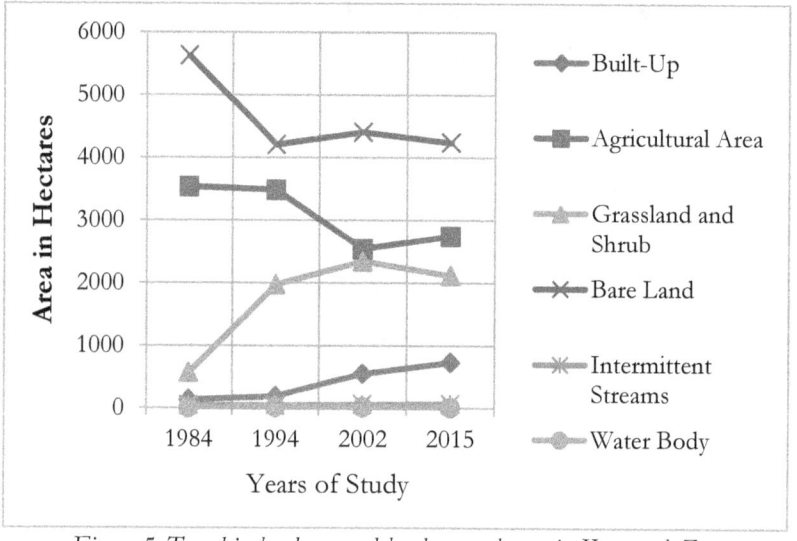

Figure 5. Trend in land use and land cover change in Keren sub-Zone.

over	Area Change in Hectares				Area Change in Percentage				Annual Rate o	
	1984-1994	1994-2002	2002-2015	1984-2015	1984-1994	1994-2002	2002-2015	1984-2015	1984-1994	1994-2002
	56.97	363.60	183.42	603.99	44.64	196.98	33.46	473.27	4.46	24.62
Area	-49.23	-946.17	205.92	-789.48	-1.39	-27.14	8.11	-22.33	-0.14	-3.39
nd	1404.63	370.98	-225.72	1549.89	248.52	18.83	-9.64	274.22	24.85	2.35
d	-1426.14	193.23	-155.43	-1391.76	-25.36	4.60	-3.54	-24.73	-2.54	0.58
nt	-0.72	14.76	6.57	20.61	-1.79	37.27	12.09	51.12	-0.18	4.66
ly	12.33	-3.42	-2.16	6.75	342.50	-21.47	-17.27	187.50	34.25	-2.68

Table 5. Land use and land cover changes.

Moreover, analysis of land use and land cover change was made using the Terrset applications of CROSSTAB and LCM modules to have an overview of the transaction among the different land use and land cover classes. A change map from 1984 to 2015 was generated by ignoring transitions of less than 10 hectares (figure 6). From the produced map it can be easily inferred that much of the change has been experienced by built-up, agricultural, grazing and shrubs and bare land in which the built-up and grazing and shrubs experienced significant gains while the bare and agricultural lands experienced major loss. Moreover, the CROSSTAB Contribution to net change in Built-Up shows that much of the contributions to the built-up expansion was made from the agricultural and bare land classes with 393 hectares and 227 hectares respectively (Table 6).

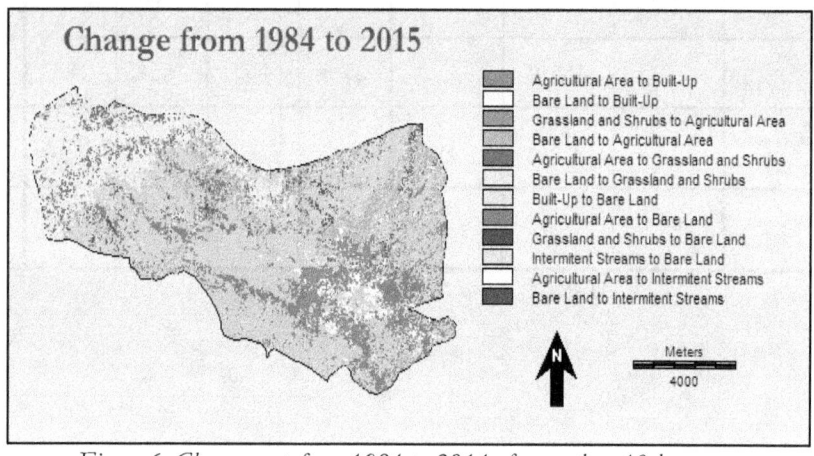

Figure 6. Change map from 1984 to 2014 of more than 10 hectares.

<table>
<tr><td rowspan="2" colspan="2"></td><td colspan="7">2015</td></tr>
</table>

		Built-Up	Agricultural Area	Grassland and Shrubs	Bare Land	Intermittent Streams	Water Body	Total
1984	Built-Up	**99.09**	1.35	0.27	26.73	0.18	0	127.62
	Agricultural Area	393.21	**1664.91**	315.54	1122.84	33.48	5.85	3535.83
	Grassland and Shrubs	2.88	82.35	**340.47**	137.34	0.27	1.89	565.2
	Bare Land	227.16	987.3	1458.63	**2934.72**	16.29	2.61	5626.71
	Intermittent Streams	9.27	8.28	0.18	11.88	**10.71**	0	40.32
	Water Body	0	2.16	0	1.44	0	**0**	3.6
	Total	731.61	2746.35	2115.09	4234.95	60.93	10.35	9899.28

Table 6. Cross-tabulation of Land Cover Classes between 1984 and 2015 (area in hectares).

C. Changes in urban landscape

The results of metric calculation for the 1984, 1994, 2002, and 2015 data to identify changes of built-up area patterns indicated the increase in CA as a result of urban sprawl from 1984 to 2015, especially during 1994 –2002 (Table 7). Increased values of CA in 1994, 2002 and 2015 also indicated the remarkable expansion of new built-up areas in the city. The urban blocks in this case, increased by 72.5% from 1984 to 1994, indicating higher level of fragmentation in the development of the built-up areas. However, it decreased significantly by 21.7% from 1994 to 2002. Moreover, it also decreased considerably by 2.8% between 2002 and 2015.

This reveals development of urban features in open spaces and it also indicates that urban growth occurred gradually in the surrounding of the existing developed areas. However, there has been an increase in the number of urban patches by 31.25% between 1984 and 2015, i.e., the values obtained for 1984 and 2015 were respectively 80 and 105, indicating that the conversion of non-built-up areas such as agricultural lands within this time span had resulted in fragmental patches of built-up areas. Furthermore, the fragmentation of built-up areas in 2015 was greater than that in 1984, reflecting the town's ongoing urbanization.

Metrics	Spatial Metrics During the Study Period				Change in Urban Structure			
	1984	1994	2002	2015	Δ%1984-1994	Δ%1994-2002	Δ%2002-2015	Δ%1984-2015
CA	127.62	184.59	548.19	731.61	44.64	196.98	33.46	473.27
NP	80.00	138.00	108.00	105.00	72.50	-21.74	-2.78	31.25
ED	6.30	9.93	15.70	18.59	57.64	58.10	18.40	195.09
LPI	0.74	1.12	4.19	5.52	52.25	272.42	31.77	647.15
ENN_MN	280.51	196.44	215.04	202.48	-29.97	9.47	-5.84	-27.82
FRAC_AM	1.21	1.23	1.2622	1.2609	1.67	2.38	-0.10	3.98
FRAC_AM*	1.36	1.33	1.33	1.30	-1.68	-0.21	-2.65	-4.48
CONTAG*	56.69	47.02	47.04	49.90	-17.06	0.05	6.08	-11.97
CLUMPY	0.65	0.61	0.78	0.81	-6.16	29.46	2.64	24.68

Table 7. Results of the analysis of urban sprawl patterns for selected metrics in Keren sub-Zone.
*Spatial metrics at landscape level.

The LPI has values from 0 to 100, with the values approaching 0 when the largest patch of the corresponding patch type is increasingly small and 100 when the entire landscape consists of a single patch of the corresponding patch type. A comparison of

LPI for built-up areas between these years revealed that the built-up areas became dominant in 2002 and 2015, with LPI values of 4.19% and 5.52%, respectively. The relatively smaller value of LPI observed for 1994, i.e., 1.12% because NP for this year was more fragmented and scattered throughout the study area. A significant increment was seen between 1994 and 2002 with a rate of change 272%. This seems to represent a considerable growth of the historical urban core. Moreover, the size of the LPI has also increased at a decreasing rate between 2002 and 2015 by 31.8%. This shows that the town is also experiencing a significant continuous (compact) development of urban features.

The ED (values ≥ 0) approaches 0 when there is no class edge in the landscape. The edge density increased by 57.76%, 58.76%, and 18.12% during the three study time spans, i.e. 1984-1994, 1994-2002, and 2002-2015 respectively. This shows an increase in the total length of the edge of the urban patches. The largest ED value (18.59 m/ha) was observed for 2015 indicating the ongoing urbanization with an increase of new built-up patches. The total length of the edge of the land use patches (urban patch) increases with an increase in the land use fragmentation and development of continuous urban features. This fact supports the idea that there is some sign of sprawling in the study area. The FRAC_AM approaches 1 for shapes with very simple perimeters such as squares and circles, and 2 for shapes with highly convoluted shapes. The FRAC_AM of built areas, however, exhibit more or less no significant change during the study period. This indicates that an increase in CA, LPI and ED, in this context, does not affect the complexity of the shape. Nevertheless, the values of FRAC_AM observed for 1994, 2002 and 2015 were relatively larger than the values for 1984, indicating that the physical shapes within built-up areas were gradually and slowly showing signs of irregularity owing to the effects of urbanization process from both the peri urban and urban areas. The ENN_MN represents the average minimum distance between the individual built areas (urban) blob and hence, it is a measure of the open space between urbanized areas. A decrease in ENN_MN by 30% between 1984 and 1994 shows a decrease in the distance between the urban patches. Nevertheless, an increase in ENN_MN by 9.5% between 1994 and 2002 shows an increment in the distance between the urban patches. Moreover, during the last temporal time span, i.e., 2002-2015, it decreased significantly by 6%. However, generally ENN_MN dipped from 1984 to 2015 by 27.82%, meaning that the space between urban neighbors is shrinking over time as a result of higher urbanization density and this indicates reductions in the distance between the built-up patches.

The contagion index describes the heterogeneity of a landscape and measures to what extent landscapes are aggregated or clumped. The decrease in the CONTAG value between 1984 and 2002 indicates a high fragmentation of the landscape. However, this value increased slightly between 2002 and 2015 (6%) showing that the fragmented urban area has become denser than the 1984–2002 period. Nevertheless, the overall drop in CONTAG values between 1984 and 2015 by 12% may have resulted from higher fragmentation due to more individual urban units. CLUMPY is a class-level only metric computed such that it ranges from -1 when the patch type is maximally disaggregated to 1 when the patch type is maximally clumped (McGarigal *et al.*, 2002). The values of clumpiness index were 0.65, 0.61, 0.78, and 0.81 during 1984, 1994, 2002 and 2015 respectively, indicating an aggregation or clumpiness of urban patches.

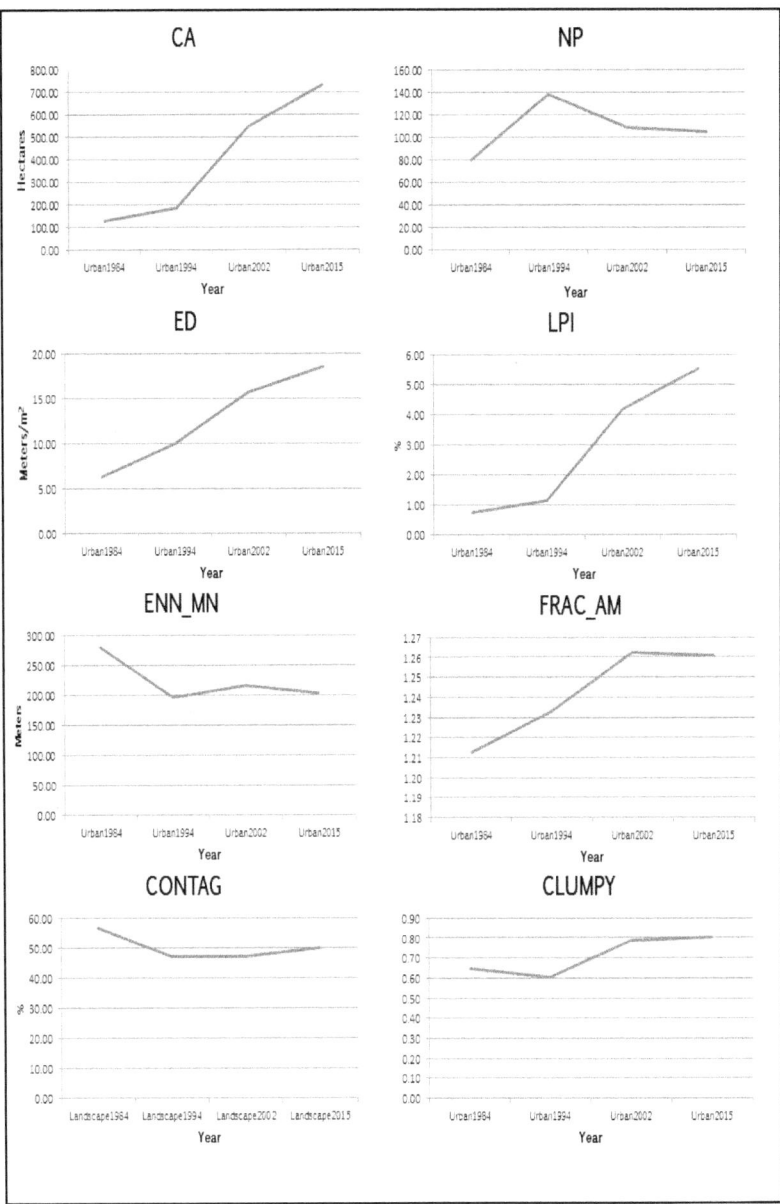

Figure 7. Temporal urban growth signatures of spatial metrics for the study area.

7. Conclusion

Time series analysis extracted from remote sensing data revealed substantial change in land use and land cover in the Keren sub-Zone since 1984. Broad-scale expansion of built-up areas at the expense of agricultural land is the most important change that reflects a long-standing human influence on natural resources. Varying rate of conversion/modification of land use and land cover in different periods is likely to occur in response to resource availability, population pressure, socio-economic and policy environments. With the population of Keren increasing as ever, the pressures on land and resources are also increasing. The urban sprawl is seen as one of the potential threats to sustainable development where urban planning with effective resource utilization and allocation of infrastructure initiatives are key concerns. The study attempted to identify such sprawls, quantified by defining few metrics. It was found out that there was urban growth in the outskirts of the sub-Zone, with the transformation of bare land and agricultural land into built-up settlements. This alarming extent and level of urban sprawl will have adverse impacts on the natural resources and land of the sub-Zone. As stated by Measho et al., (2019) the study area is located along the area where there is extreme meteorological drought. Hence the high level of sprawling combined with other numerous environmental problems the region is facing like the frequent occurrence of drought, expansion of desertification, deforestation, and soil erosion (Teklay, 1999; Nyssen, Poesen and Moeyersen, 2004; Ogbazghi and Bein, 2006; Tekeste, Habtzghi, and Stroosnijder, 2007; Ghebrezgabher, Yang and Yang, 2014; Ghebrezghiabher et al., 2019) may cause a severe consequence on the surrounding ecosystem in general and agricultural sector in particular. The combined application of geographic information systems, remote sensing, and statistical modeling techniques proved to be a useful and efficient approach for the assessment and modeling of the trends and patterns of sprawl for the Keren town.

Acknowledgements

The study was conduct as a part of the M.Sc. program in Geoinformatics at Adi QeyyiH College of Arts and Social Sciences, Eritrea, implemented through the GIERI project (Strengthening Geoinformatics Teaching and Research Capacity in Eritrea Higher Education Institutes, https://blogs.helsinki.fi/gieriproject/). This study was financed by the development cooperation funds of the Ministry for Foreign Affairs of Finland. The authors extend their thanks to Adi QeyyiH College of Arts and Social Sciences, University of Helsinki, Finnish National Agency for Education, and National Higher Education and Research Institute of Eritrea. Moreover, the authors want to extend their utmost gratitude to GIERI project director Prof. Petri Pellikka and GIERI project coordinator Mr. Pekka Hurskainen from University of Helsinki and Dr. Weldetnsae Tewolde from College of Arts and Social Sciences.

References

Abiel, Y. (2018). Urban vulnerability to poverty: Asmara's poor in perspective. In Zemenfes Tsige, Saleh Mahmud Idris, Yonas Mesfun, Senai Woldeab, & Gebreberhan Ogubazghi, (Eds.). *International Conference on Eritrean Studies: July 20-22, 2016: Proceedings*, Volume II. (pp. 987-1015). Asmara, Eritrea: NCHE.

Araya Y. H., & Cabral P. (2010). Analysis and modeling of urban land cover change in Setúbal and Sesimbra, Portugal. *Remote Sensing*. Vol. 2, 1549-1563.

Araya, Y. H., & Hergarten, C. (2008). A comparison of pixel and object-based land cover classification: A case study of Asmara, Eritrea. *Geo-environment and landscape evolution III*, i1): 233-243.

Benz, U. C., Hofmann, P., Willhauck, G., Lingenfelder, I., & Heynen, M. (2004). Multi-resolution, object-oriented fuzzy analysis of remote sensing data for GIS-ready information. *ISPRS Journal of Photogrammetry & Remote Sensing, 58* (3 & 4), 239-258.

Boerma, P. (2012). Myths, memories and metaphors: recollecting landscape change in the Eritrean highlands. *Journal of Eastern African Studies*, 6(2), 246-269.

Brink, A. B., Bodart, C., Brodsky, L., Defourney, P., Ernst, C., Donney, F., Lupi, A., & Tuckova, K. (2014). Anthropogenic pressure in East Africa – Monitoring 20 years of land cover changes by means of medium resolution satellite data. *International Journal of Applied Earth Observation and Geoinformation*, 28(1), 60-69.

Cohen, W. B., & Goward, S. N. (2004). Landsat's role in ecological applications of remote sensing. *BioScience, 54*(6), 535-545.

Department of Urban Development, Ministry of Public Works. (2005). housing/urban development policy report.

Ghebrezgabher M. G., Yang T., & Yang X. (2014). Remote Sensing and GIS analysis of deforestation and desertification in central highland and eastern region of Eritrea (1972-2014). *International Journal of Sciences: Basic and Applied Research*, 18(2): 161-176.

Ghebrezgabher M. G., Yang T., Yang X., & Congqiang, W. (2019). Assessment of desertification in Eritrea: land degradation based on Landsat images. *Journal of Arid Land*, 11(3): 319-331.

GlobCover (2009): Land Cover Map, ESA 2009 and UCLouvain.

Hayes, D. J. & Cohen, W. B. (2007). Spatial, spectral and temporal patterns of tropical forest cover change as observed with multiple scales of optical satellite data. *Remote Sensing of Environment*, *106*(1), 1-16.

Herold, M., Couclelis, H & Clarke, K. C. (2005). The role of spatial metrics in the analysis and modeling of urban land use change. *Computers, Environment and Urban Systems*, *29*(4): 369-399.

Herold, M., Goldstein, N. C., & Clarke, K. C., (2003). The spatiotemporal form of urban growth: measurement, analysis and modeling. *Remote Sensing of Environment*, 86(1), 286-302.

Im, J., Jensen, J. R. & Tullis, J. A. (2008). Object-based change detection using correlation image analysis and image segmentation. *International Journal of Remote Sensing*, 29(2), 399-423.

inta, M., Kibret, K., Thorne, P., Nigussie, T., & Nigatu, L. (2018). Land use and land cover dynamics in Dendi-Jeldu hilly-mountainous areas in the central Ethiopian highlands. *Geoderma*, *314*(1), 27-36.

Jacob, M., Frankl, A., Hurni, H., Lanckriet, S., Ridder, M. D., Guyassa, E., Beeckman, H., & Nyssen, J. (2017). Land cover dynamics in the Simien Mountains (Ethiopia), half a century after establishment of the National Park. *Regional Environmental Change*, *17*(1), 777-787.

Jensen, J. R. (2005). *Introductory digital image processing: a remote sensing perspective* (3rd ed.). New Jersey: Prentice Hall.

Jensen, R. R., Gatrel, J. D., & Mclean, D.D. (2007). *Geo-spatial technologies in urban environments: Policy, practice and pixels* (2nd ed.). Berlin, Heidelberg, New York: Springer.

Ji, W., Ma, J., Twibell, R. W., & Underhill, K. (2006). Characterizing urban sprawl using multi-stage remote sensing images and landscape metrics. *Computers, Environment and Urban Systems*, *30*(6), 861-879.

Keren sub-Zone (2017). sub-Zone Statistics office, Keren.

Lambin, E. F., Turner, B. L., Geist, H. J., Agbola, S. B., Angelsen, A., Bruce, J. W., Coomes, O. T., Dirzo, R., Fischer, G., Folke, C., George, P.S., Homewood, K., Imbernon, J., Leemans, R.,

Li, X., Moran, E. F., Mortimore, M., Ramakrishnan, P. S., Richards, J. F., Skånes, H., Steffen, W., Stone, G. D., Svedin, U., Veldkamp, T. A., Vogel, C., & Xu J. (2001). The causes of land-use and land-cover change: moving beyond the myths. *Global Environmental Change, 11*(4), 261-269.

Li, X.; & Yeh, A. G.-O. (2004). Analyzing spatial restructuring of land use patterns in a fast growing region using remote sensing and GIS. *Landscape and Urban Planning, 69*(1), 335-354.

Lilesand, T. M, Kiefer, R. W., & Chipman J. W. (2015). *Remote sensing and image interpretation* (7th ed.). New York: John Wiley and Sons, Inc.

Lu, D., Mausel, P., Bronddizios, E., & Morain, E. (2004). Change detection techniques. *International Journal of Remote Sensing, 25*(12), 2365-2407.

Masek, J. G., Lindsay, F. E & Goward, S. N. (2000). Dynamics of urban growth in the Washington DC metropolitan area, 1973-1996, from Landsat observations. *International Journal of Remote Sensing, 21*(18), 3473-3486.

McGarigal, K., Cushman, S., Neel, M. & Ene, E. (2002). FRAGSTATS: spatial pattern analysis program for categorical maps. Master's thesis, University of Massachusetts, Amherst.

Measho, S., Chen, B., Trisurat, Y., Pellikka, P., Guo, L., Arunyawat, S., Tuankrua, V., Ogbazghi, W., & Yemane, T. (2019). Spatio-temporal analysis of vegetation dynamics as a response to climate variability and drought patterns in the semiarid region, Eritrea. *Remote Sensing, 11*(6), 724-747.

Megahed, Y., Cabral, P., Silva, J., & Caetano, M. (2015). Land cover mapping analysis and urban growth modelling using remote sensing techniques in Greater Cairo region – Egypt. *ISPRS International Journal of Geo-Information, 4*(1): 1750-1769.

Ministry of Agriculture (MoA), State of Eritrea. (2002). The national action program for Eritrea to combat desertification and mitigate the effects of drought (NAP). Asmara, Eritrea.

Ministry of Land, Water and Environment (MLWE), State of Eritrea. (2012). Eritrea's five years action plan (2011-2015) for The Great Green Wall Initiative (GGWI) (Draft). Asmara, Eritrea.

MoA, (2002). The national action program for Eritrea to combat desertification and mitigate the effects of drought (NAP). Asmara, Eritrea.

Neteler, M., Bowman, M. H., Landa, M., and Metz, M., (2012). GRASS GIS: a multi-purpose Open Source GIS. *Environmental Modelling & Software*, *31*(1), 124-130.

Nyssen J., Poesen J., Moeyersons J., Deckers, J., Haile, M., Lang, A. (2004). Human impact on the environment in the Ethiopian and Eritrean highlands–a state of the art. *Earth-Science Reviews*, *64*(3–4): 273-320.

Ogbazghi W., & Bein E. (2006). Assessment of non-wood forest products and their role in the livelihoods of rural communities in the Gash-Barka region, Eritrea. Drylands Coordination Group Report (No. 40). Oslo, Norway.

Padmanaban, R., Bhowmik, A.k., Cabral, P., Zamyatin, A., Almegdadi, O., & Wang, S. (2017). Modelling urban sprawl using remotely sensed data: A case study of Chennai city, Tamilnadu. *Entropy*, *19*(4), 163-167.

Shalaby, A., & Tateishi, R. (2007). Remote sensing and GIS for mapping and monitoring land cover and land-use changes in the Northwestern coastal zone of Egypt. *Applied Geography*, *27*(1), 28-41.

Tekeste M., Habtzghi D H, & Stroosnijder L. (2007). Soil strength assessment using threshold probability approach on soils from three agro-ecological zones in Eritrea. *Biosystems Engineering*, *98*(4), 470-478.

Teklay M. (1999). Earth science education in Eritrea. *Journal of African Earth Sciences*, *28*(4), 805-810.

Tewolde, M. G. (2011). Urban sprawl analysis and modeling in Asmara, Eritrea: Application of geospatial tools. M.Sc. thesis, Institute for Geoinformatics (ifgi): University of Münster.

Tewolde, M. G., & Cabral, P. (2011). Urban sprawl analysis and modeling in Asmara, Eritrea. *Remote Sensing*, *3*(1), 2148-2165.

Turner, B. L., Meyer, W. B., & Skole, D. L. (1994). Global land-use land-cover change—towards an integrated study. *Ambio*, *23*(1), 91-95.

Weng, Q. (2012). Remote sensing of impervious surfaces in the urban areas: Requirements, methods, and trends. *Remote Sensing of Environment*, *117*(1), 34-49.

Weng, Y. (2007). Spatiotemporal changes of landscape pattern in response to urbanization. *Landscape and Urban Planning*, *81*(4): 341-353.

Yang, L., Xian, G., Klaver, J. M., & Deal, B. (2003). Urban land-cover change detection through sub-pixel imperviousness mapping using remotely sensed data. *Photogrammetric Engineering & Remote Sensing*, *69*(9), 1003-1010.

Zhu, Z., Woodcock, C. E., & Olofsson, P. (2012). Continuous monitoring of forest disturbance using all available Landsat imagery. *Remote Sensing of Environment*, *122*(1), 75-91.

Distribution of Mangrove Forest along the Eritrean Red Sea Coast Using Sentinel-2 Data (2017)

Elias Gebreluul[1] and Zekeria Abdelkerim[2]

Abstract

Little information is available regarding the surface coverage and distribution of the Eritrean Red Sea mangroves. The present study was performed by using Sentinel-2 data. The results showed that, 6571 ha in the Eritrean Red Sea coast are covered by mangrove forest. This is due to the afforestation projects and natural replenishment of mangrove forest. The presence of few coastal population and urban development projects along the coast plus the traditional beliefs of the Afar people on protecting the plant and animals present in the coast have also played an important role in maintaining and expanding mangrove along the Eritrean Red Sea. However, coastal development and its related activities may represent future threat for mangrove ecosystem unless mangrove conservation receives prominent attention.

Keywords: Eritrea; mangroves; Sentinel-2 data; supervised classification; maximum likelihood classifier; accuracy assessment.

1. Introduction

Mangroves are defined as 'woody plants' that grow in tropical and subtropical latitudes along the land-sea interface, bays, estuaries, lagoons, and backwaters. Their global distribution is believed to be delimited by major ocean currents and the 20°C isotherm of seawater in winter. The forests are typically distributed from mean sea level to highest spring tide (Giri *et al.*, 2010). An increase in latitude is reflected in lower species richness and tree height

[1] Lecturer, Department of Biology, Mai Nefhi College of Science, Eritrea. Email: elumbf@yahoo.com/eliasgis2018@gmail.com.
[2] Associate Professor, Department of Biology, Mai Nefhi College of Science, Eritrea. Email: z-a-zekeria@yahoo.com.

(Duke, 1998; Spalding, 2010). Beyond their latitudinal limits, mangroves are replaced by salt marshes in their tidal position with a limited zone of co-occurrence. Temperature and aridity are key factors in explaining why mangroves reach latitudinal limits in the northern and southern hemispheres (Duke, 1998). They grow in areas of high salinity, high temperature and extreme tidal zones, which have high sedimentation rates and muddy anaerobic soils (Giri et al., 2011). Mangrove forests are distributed in intertidal zones where ocean, fresh water and brackish water meet in approximately between 30^0N and 30^0S latitude (Giri et al., 2011; Donato et al., 2011).

Eritrea is located in the Horn of Africa between 12^0 22' and 18^0 02' north and between 36^0 26' and $43^0$13' east serving as a bridge between the rest of Africa and the Middle East and the Gulf States. Eritrea has a total land area of 124,300 km². It is situated along the important Red Sea shipping route connecting the Mediterranean Sea with the Indian Ocean. It has about 1350 km of mainland coastline and over 360 islands which add another 1950 km of shoreline. The country exhibits a varied topography, rainfall and climate with altitude that ranges from 120 mts. below sea level to over 3000 mts. above sea level. The continental shelf extends from the coast to a maximum distance of 120 km east of Massawa, narrowing to about 20 km in the north and south of the country (De Grissac & Negusie, 2007).

The climatic regimes of Eritrea follow the geography. The low eastern coastal zone is the hottest with little rainfall, an average of 200mm, and temperature between 30°C and 39°C, occasionally higher during the hot season (June to September) and 25°C to 32°C during the cooler season (October to May). The coastal area is also occasionally subject to dust storms and strong wind during the summer. There is no permanent river that drains into the Red Sea coast of Eritrea, only a number of dry river beds ("wadis") that experience occasional flash flooding that reaches the coast (De Grissac & Negusie, 2007).

The climate of Eritrea ranges from hot and arid adjacent to the Red Sea to temperate in the highlands and sub-humid in isolated micro-catchments of the eastern escarpment. Most part of the country (70%) is classified as hot to very hot with mean annual temperature of more than 27°C, about 25% of the area as warm to mild with a mean temperature of about 22°C, and the remaining parts (5%) as cool with a mean annual temperature of less than 19 °C. The total annual rainfall increases from the north to south and varies from less than 200 mm in the northwestern lowlands to more than 700 mm in the southwestern lowlands. Besides, the amount of rainfall also increases with altitude. While the coastal lowlands are very dry, some areas on the eastern escarpment get more than 1000 mm of rain. As to areas covered by the different rainfall regimes, about 50% of the country receives less than 300 mm, 40% between 300 and 600 mm and about 10% more than 600 mm of rain per annum (FAO, 1994; Haile *et al.*, 1998).

According to De Grissac & Negusie (2007, p. 37) "about 380 km^2 of the Eritrean mainland and islands coastlines are occupied by mangrove forests". Of the seven mangrove species present in the Red Sea area, three are present in Eritrea, on the mainland and on numerous islands. These species are *Avicennia marina*, *Rhizophora mucronata* and *Ceriops tagal*.

Mangrove forests are among the most productive and biologically important ecosystems of the world because they provide important and unique ecosystem goods and services to human society and coastal and marine ecosystems. The forests help stabilize shorelines and reduce the devastating impact of natural disasters such as tsunamis and hurricanes. They also provide breeding and nursing grounds for marine species; they are also used for food, medicine, fuel and building materials by local communities. Mangroves are able to maintain the water quality by acting as biological filters, separating sediments and nutrients in polluted coastal areas. Mangroves, including associated soils, could sequester approximately 22.8 million metric tons of carbon each year. Covering only 0.1% of the earth's continental surface, the forests account for 11% of the total input of terrestrial carbon into the ocean (Jennerjahn & Ittekot, 2002) and 10% of the terrestrial dissolved organic carbon exported to the oceans (Dittmar et al., 2006). The rapid disappearance and degradation of mangroves could have negative consequences for transfer of materials into the marine systems and influence the atmospheric composition and climate. Mangrove forests have huge value. An estimated $1.6 trillion per year value-service is delivered from mangrove ecosystem mainly in terms of coastal protection, food, nursery area, nesting and firewood production (Costanza et al., 1997; Cavanaugh et al., 2014).

Throughout their areal extent, however, these habitats are in a state of decline. According to Giri et al., (2010) services offered by the mangrove forest may possibly be lost in the coming 100 years. If the present rate of loss contiNe'us, as a consequence, important ecosystem goods and services provided by mangrove forests will be diminished or lost.

According to Hailemichael (2015, p. 7), "African mangrove cover approximately 4.6 million ha of which 3.1 million ha is found along western African coastlines, 0.33 million ha in Madagascar and 1.14 million ha in eastern Africa". Of the latter, approximately 10,200 ha (102 km^2) area is found in the Eritrea Red Sea Coast and Islands (Spalding & Kainuma, 2010). However, FAO (2005) and Fatoyinbo et al. (2013) put the mangrove cover in Eritrea at around 6400 and 4900 ha respectively. On the other hand, De Grissac and Negusie (2007) estimate that about 380 km^2 of the Eritrean mainland and islands coastlines to be covered by mangrove forests.

Despite their importance and significance, our understanding of the present status and distributions of the mangrove forests of the Eritrean Red Sea coast is inadequate. There are few reports which have information related to mangrove forests of the Eritrean Red Sea. However, the estimate of mangrove cover obtained from these reports is contradictory (inconsistent). Observations on the mangrove coverage around the Massawa coast started in 2007. Results from previous studies show that there was a decrease in mangrove cover in some areas while in other areas increase in the mangrove coverage was recorded. So, the objective of this study is to collect comprehensive and updated data on the cover of mangrove along the entire Eritrean coast.

Therefore, taking the above considerations, this study was initiated to investigate the distribution of mangrove forests along the Eritrean Red Sea coast in 2017 using Sentinel-2 images from Copernicus Sentinel-2 data.

2. Materials and Methods

A. The study area

The study area covers the whole of the Eritrean coast of the Red Sea from Ras Kasar in the North ($38°6'64":17°99'482"$) to Ras Dumera in the South ($43°12'12":12°70'83"$) (Fig. 1). Distribution of mangrove is not uniform throughout the Eritrean coast thus the detailed study was conducted in three sites that have high mangrove cover. These sites are:

- Southern study area extending from the Eritrean border with Djibouti up to Tio (including Rastarma, Assab and Barasole);
- Central study area extending from Tio to Marsa Mubarek (including Dahlak Archipelago, Ghelaelo-Tio, Zula, and Massawa); and

- Northern study area extending from Marsa Mubarek until the northern border of Eritrea with the Sudan (Berite, Marsa Mubarek and Marsa Ibrahim).

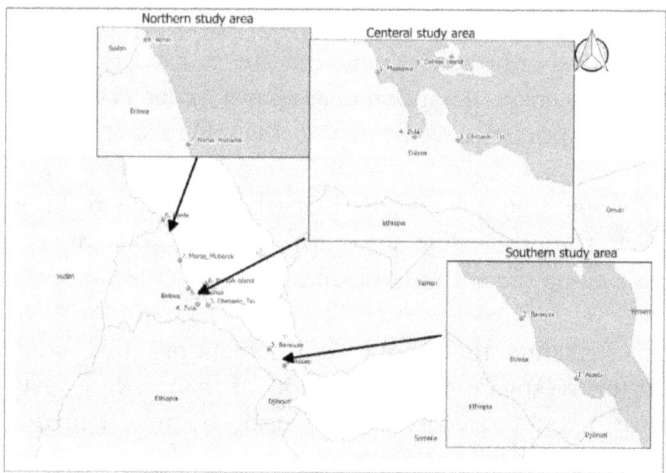

Figure1. Study area along Eritrean coast.

B. Methodology

i. Remote sensing data

In this study Sentinel-2 images from Copernicus Sentinel-2 data were acquired and analyzed using QGIS software. Sentinel-2 images were used to analyze and to map the distribution of mangrove coverage (area) in 2017. In this study, it was difficult to obtain all of the Sentinel-2 images at the same season and year (2017), because some images were obscured by cloud cover. In such cases, cloud-free images of 2017 were used. Since mangroves are evergreen, their leaf phenology and spectral reflectance remains more or less constant throughout the year, so seasonality does not have any effect on image acquisition. The following steps were followed in analyzing the satellite images.

ii. *Atmospheric correction*

First, the acquired Sentinel-2 images are only geometrically corrected, so Cosine of Solar Zenith Angle (COST) relative correction method (Chavez, 1996) was applied to correct atmospheric effects and to convert pixel values to Surface Reflectance.

iii. *Image composites*

After atmospheric correction, individual bands of Sentinel-2 images were stacked together to create multi-band composites for supervised image classification. False Color Composites were generated using bands Blue, Green, Red, NIR and SWIR for visualization purpose.

iv. *Image masking*

At last, mangrove masks for every study area were delineated by focusing on potential mangrove vegetation sites along the coast and islands. All multi-band composite images were clipped to study area extent using these polygon masks.

v. *Ground reference data*

Field ground reference data was collected starting from April up to December 2017. Location and Geo-tagged photos of mangrove were collected from the field using Garmin Oregon 650 GPS hand-held device. These points were supplemented with points collected from high-resolution satellite images from Google Earth. A total of 4900 points were collected, of which 70% were used for training of the classification algorithm and 30% for accuracy assessment as independent dataset.

vi. Image processing

Supervised classification aims to classify image pixels into a defined number of classes based on the pixel values. There are many different algorithms used to rate the degree of similarity. In the present study, Maximum Likelihood Classification was used. The maximum likelihood algorithm uses a parametric logic which assumes that the data is normally distributed and the classes are trained based on the probability density function (Richards & Jia, 2005). The probability of each pixel belonging to any particular class was calculated, and then the pixel was assigned to the class with the highest probability as mangrove and non-mangrove class.

vii. Accuracy assessment

After the classification, the accuracy, reliability and degree of error was assessed by comparing the classification result to an independent dataset. Usually, accuracy assessment was performed with the calculation of an error matrix, which is a table that compares map information with reference data (i.e., ground truth data) for a number of sample areas (Congalton & Green, 2009). An error matrix is a very effective way to represent an accuracy assessment because the accuracy of each category is clearly described, along with both the errors of commission (i.e., User's Accuracy) and the errors of omission (i.e., Producer's Accuracy). The error matrix can also be used to calculate other accuracy metrics, most notably Kappa statistics. The kappa statistics shows that the probability of an agreement that could be expected to present by chance (Yuan F, 2005), and the value ranges from +1.0 to -1.0, that is, it ranges, respectively from strong agreement to poor agreement.

3. Results

The image of the study area is classified into Mangrove and Non-Mangrove categories based on the supervised classification. FCC (732) RGB composite bands for Sentinel-2 gave healthy green vegetation in reddish tones. Mangrove distribution was mapped and found as patches and forest form. Compared with Northern coast, the Central and Southern coast have higher mangrove cover. Detailed data of mangrove cover for the three sites is given in Table 1 below and the sentinel-2 image result of the distribution of mangrove forest along the Eritrean Red Sea was given in figure 2 and Table 2.

Satellite system	Study site	Date	Resolution	Projection
S2A	Berite	12-01-2017	10,20 M	WGS84/zone37
S2A	Marsa Mubarek	12-01-2017	10,20 M	WGS84/zone37
S2A	Barasole	16-01-2017	10,20 M	WGS84/zone38
S2A	Assab	19-01-2017	10,20 M	WGS84/zone38
S2A	Zula	19-01-2017	10,20 M	WGS84/zone37
S2A	Dahlak	19-01-2017	10,20 M	WGS84/zone37
S2A	Zula	11-02-2017	10,20 M	WGS84/zone37
S2A	Zula-Marsa Mubarek	11-02-2017	10,20 M	WGS84/zone37
S2A	Ghelaelo-Tio	28-02-2017	10,20 M	WGS84/zone37
S2A	Dahlak	28-02-2017	10,20 M	WGS84/zone37

Table 1. Satellite image data used in the study areas, date of acquisition, resolution and projection used.

Study area	Study Sites	GPS location	Mangrove cover (Ha)
Southern Study Area	Assab	918463N,1432558E	1724
	Barasole	845711N,1507369E	336
Central Study Area	Ghelaelo-Tio	642939N,1660702E	2396
	Zula	578599N,1695516E	159
	Massawa	549849N,1724904E	47
	Dahlak island	595287N,1752886E	1403
Northern Study Area	Marsa Mubarek	522230N,1828871E	466
	Berite	458039N,1982719E	40
Total in ha			6571

Table 2. List of study sites, their location and mangrove cover in 2017.

According to the classified images of all of the study areas, the mangrove cover was 6571 ha. The result also revealed that high mangrove cover was observed in the Central and the Southern study areas compared to the Northern study area (Figures 2 -11).

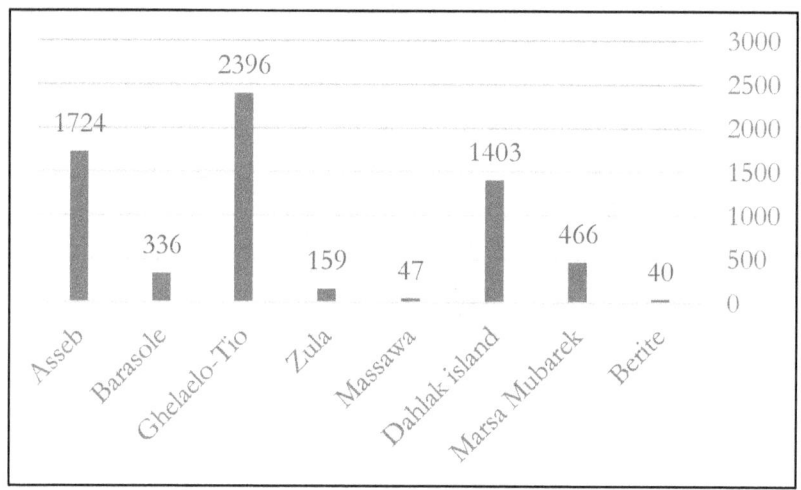

Figure 2. Mangrove cover in all the study sites in 2017.

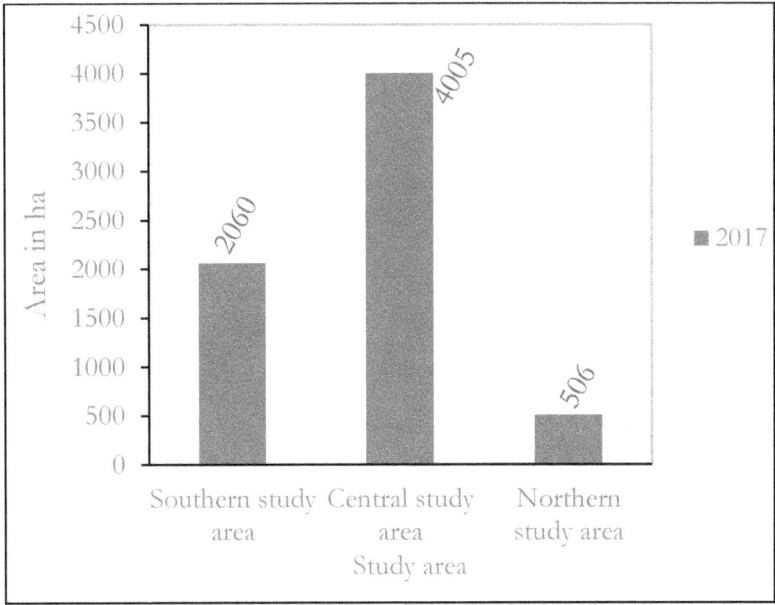

Figure 3. Mangrove cover in Southern, Central and Northern study areas in 2017.

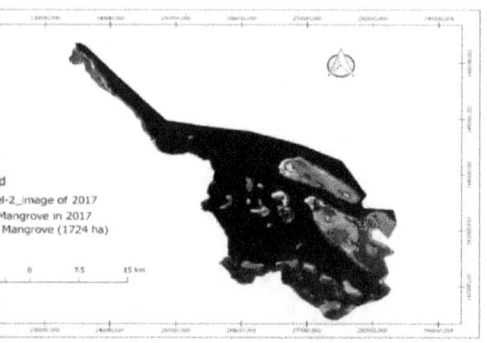

Figure 4. Mangrove of Assab area in 2017.

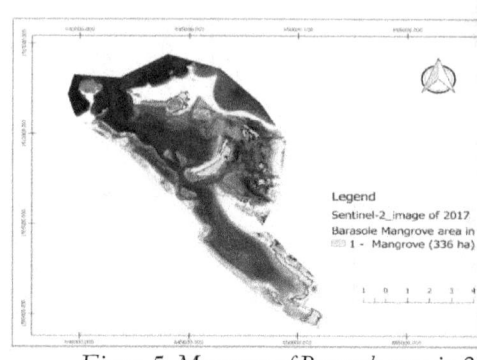

Figure 5. Mangrove of Barasole area in 20

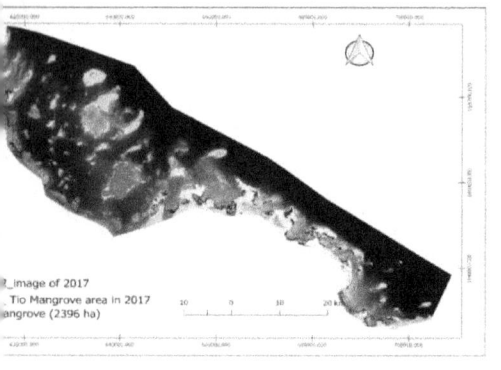

re 6. Mangrove of Ghelaelo-Tio area in 2017.

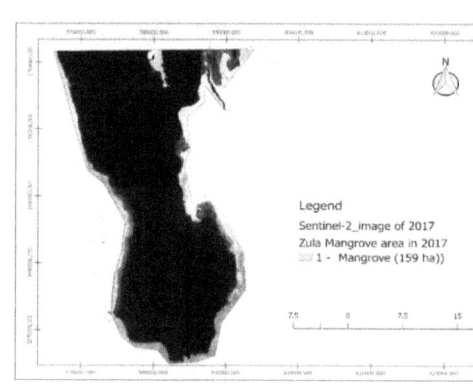

Figure 7. Mangrove of Zula area in 201

Elias Gebreluul and Zekeria Abdulkerim

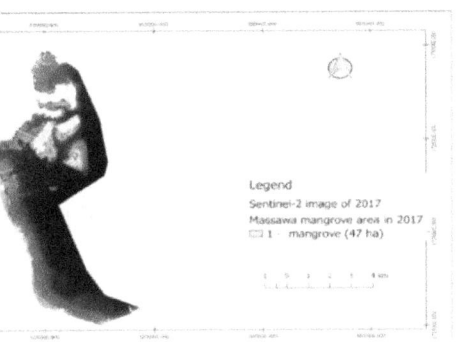

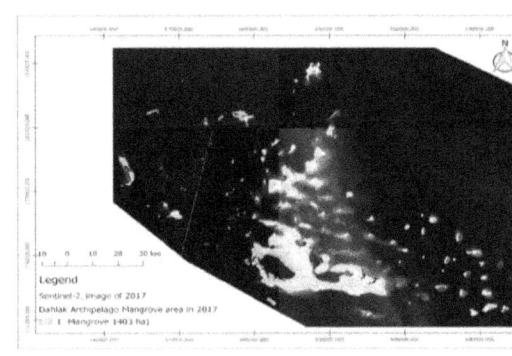

re 8. *Mangrove of Massawa area in 2017.*

Figure 9. Mangrove of Dahlak area in 2017.

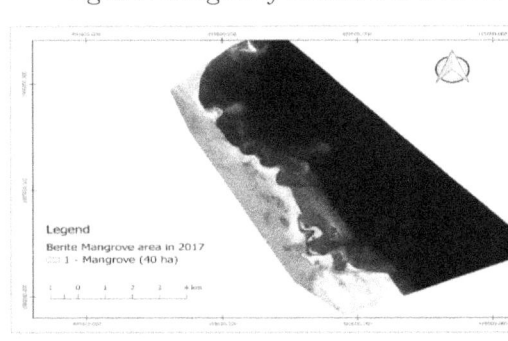

10. Mangrove of Marsa Mubarek in 2017.

Figure 11. Mangrove of Berite area in 2017.

47

The weighted overall accuracy of the classified and the reference data was 96%. This result reveals that, there was a strong agreement between the reference and the classified satellite data because kappa value was 0.82 (Table 3).

Study area	2017		2017
	Area(ha)	Overall accuracy (%)	Kappa value
Assab	1724	95%	0.89
Barasole	336	96%	0.9
Ghelaelo-Tio	2396	97%	0.47
Zula	159	79%	0.52
Massawa	47	95%	0.82
Dahlak	1403	96%	0.92
Marsa_Mubarek	466	99%	1
Berite	40	100%	1
Total	6571		
Weighed overall accuracy		95.8%	0.82

Table 3. Weighted over all accuracy of mangrove cover along the study areas.

4. Discussion

The study found out that approximately 6571 hectares of mangrove forest was distributed along the Eritrean Red Sea coast (Table 2). This is higher than mangrove area covered in neighboring countries such as Sudan (500 ha), much higher than Egypt (512 ha) and Djibouti (1000 ha) (FAO, 2007).

The result of the present study indicates that highest mangrove cover is found in the central study area (61%), followed by southern study area (31%), and lowest is found in the Northern study area (8%) (Table 2). This may be because all of the mangrove forests are found in protected environments (such as bays, lagoons, narrow channels, and inland face of offshore islands), higher rainfall and the rivers that flows into the sea, more nutrient and less saline waters along the Southern and Central

Eritrean Red Sea coast as compared to the northern study area. Wider continental shelf was also found in the Central study area as compared to the Southern study area. This gives an advantage and may have resulted in denser mangrove along central eritrean Red Sea coast.

As a projection of the Indian Ocean, water exchange is more pronounced due to monsoon winds in southern part than in the northern part (Naheed, 2015). As a result, a less saline water of the Red Sea combined with nutrient rich water from the Indian Ocean give an advantage in having denser mangrove along southern Eritrean Red Sea coast.

The result of this study also showed that there is an increase in the mangrove cover in the Central study area in 2017. This could be due to rapid decrease in the sea cucumber fisheries harvest that was observed in the central part of the Eritrean Red Sea. There is a decrease in the mangrove cover in the Central study area from 1998-2006. This could be due to deforestation of the mangrove forest, which was used for processing of sea cucumber fisheries (National Fisheries Corporation, 2018; Mahta et al., 2014). The central and the southern eritrean Red Sea coasts have many rivers that flow into the sea bringing more nutrients into the mangrove habitat, which may also play a great role in increasing the mangrove forest of the coast (De Grissac & Negusie, 2007).

At present, due to unplanned urban and coastal development projects (like road construction along the Massawa-Assab axis), the mangrove ecosystem is threatened by land based activities. Mangrove forest in Wadi area along the coast is becoming stressed due to fresh water being blocked or diverted for agriculture. This results in high salt concentration in the mangrove soil which leads to mangrove loss (DoE, 2014). There are also many villages in the central and southern Eritrean Red Sea coast where the villagers have large number of camels as compared to the northern Eritrean Red Sea coasts. The mangroves of this region are more affected by camel browsing, goats, cattle and sheep (Zekeria, 2018). In some areas browsing by camel is a great threat to mangrove trees and it is causing some damage like killing of seedlings, pneumatophores and saplings. In addition to the direct grazing of the animals, collecting leaves and seeds for animals feed were observed during the present study (Ministry of Agriculture Northern Red Sea, 2010 and personal observation).

The result also revealed that, only 47 ha of mangrove coverage was found around the Massawa coast. This could be due to lack of guidelines that protect coastal areas from coastal development projects along the coast (De Grissac & Negusie, 2007).

According to this study, 6571 ha of mangrove forest is found in Eritrea. This could be due to, the restoration and plantation of mangroves undertaken by the Ministry of Marine Resources along the Eritrean coast. Recently, the Ministry has planted mangroves in Kormelil, Dahlak Kebir, Beradu, and Dessie islands in addition to the natural replenishment of mangrove propagules (seeds) in its natural environment. The closure of Sea Cucumber fisheries in Eritrea starting from 2007-2012 and the rapid decrease in the quantity of sea cucumber fisheries harvested from the Eritrea Red Sea after 2013 could also be the main reason for the increase in the mangrove coverage (National Fisheries Corporation, 2018; Mahta et al., 2014). In Eritrea, a large part of the mangrove forest can be considered well-protected because they are situated in areas with low population density and where access is difficult (especially the mangrove which are found in the island). There was also no urban development activity along the coast in the past 10 years. Considerable pressures exist in other parts of the coast, related to intensive use of mangrove wood and grazing by camels (DOE, 2014). The traditional beliefs of the Afar people against cutting trees and killing of wild animals has also contributed to the increase of mangroves along the Eritrean coast of the Red Sea.

According to the people's belief, cutting the entire canopy of a tree would entail anger and wrath from heaven. They also believe that the killing of wild animals in particular the grazers and browsers is the direct cause for drought. According to their world perspective, 'God gives rain for the sake of wild animals, and if all of the wild animals are decimated, there will be no rain' (De Grissac & Negusie, 2007).

5. Conclusion

In summary, the results presented here showed that 6571 ha of mangrove area was found along the Eritrean Red Sea during the present study (in 2017). This expansion is due to afforestation projects and natural replenishment of mangroves. The presence of few coastal population as well as the presence of few urban and coastal development project along the coast and the traditional beliefs of the Afar people on protecting the plant and animals present in coast have also played an important role in maintaining and expanding mangrove along the Eritrean Red Sea.

References

Cavanaugh, K. C, Kellner, J. R, Forde, A. J, Gruner, D. S, Parker, J. D, Rodriguez, W & Feller, I. C. (2014). Poleward expansion of mangroves is a threshold response to decreased frequency of extreme cold events. *Proceedings of the National Academy of Sciences of the United State of America, 111*(2), 723-727.

Chavez, P. S(1996). Image-Based atmospheric corrections - Revisited and improved. *Photogrammetric Engineering and Remote Sensing, 62*, 1025-1036.

Coastal Marine and Island Biodiversity Conservation Project, 22. UNDP-Eritrea.

Congalton, R. & Green, K. (2009). *Assessing the accuracy of remotely sensed data: Principles and practices* (2nd ed.). Boca Raton: CRC Press.

Costanza, R., d'Arge, R., de Groot, R., Farberk, S., Grasso, M., Hannon, B., Limburg, K., Naeem, S., O'Neill, R. V., Paruelo, J., Raskin, R. G., Sutton, P., can den Belt, M. (1997). The value of the world's ecosystem services and natural capital. *Nature, 387*(5), 253-260.

De Grissac, A. J., and Negussie, K. (eds.) (2007). *State of the Coast Eritrea, 2006-2007, Eritrea's coastal marine and island biodiversity conservation project*, UNDP-Eritrea.

Department of the Environment (DoE), Ministry of Land, Water and Environment, State of Eritrea (2014). The 5th National report on the implementation of the United Nation Convention of Biological Diversity (UNCBD). Asmara, Eritrea.

Dittmar, T., Hertkorn, N., Kattner, G. & Lara, R. J. (2006). Mangroves, a major source of dissolved organic carbon to the oceans. *Global Biogeochemical Cycles, 20*(1), 1-7.

Donato, D. C., Kauffman, J. B., Murdiyarso, D., Kurnianto, S., Stidham, M., & Kanninen, M. (2011). Mangroves among the most carbon-rich forests in the tropics. *Nature Geoscience, 4*(5), 293-297.

Duke, N. C., Ball, M. C., & Ellison, J. C. (1998). Factors influencing biodiversity and distributional gradients in mangroves. *Global Ecology and Biogeography Letters, 7*, 27-47.

FAO (2005). Global Forest Resources Assessment 2005: Main report. FAO Forestry Paper. FAO, Rome.

FAO (2007). The world's mangroves 1980-2005. FAO Forestry Paper 153. FAO, Rome.

FAO [Food and Agriculture Organization of the United Nations] (1994). Mangrove forest management guidelines. FAO Forestry Paper 117. FAO, Rome.

Fatoyinbo, T. E., & Simard, M. (2013). Height and biomass of mangroves in Africa from ICESat/GLAS and SRTM. *International Journal of Remote Sensing, 34*(2), 668-681.

Giri, C., Ochieng, E., Tieszen, L. L., Zhu, Z., Singh, A., Loveland, T. R., Masek, J., & Duke, N. C. (2010). Status and distribution of mangrove forests of the world using earth observation satellite data. *Global Ecology and Biogeography, 20*(1), 154-159.

Hailemichael, M. T. (2015). *Mangrove forest extent and status along the Eritrean Red Sea coast.* Master thesis, Department of Biology, University of Bergen.

Jennerjahn, T. C. & Ittekot, V. (2002). Relevance of mangroves for the production and deposition of organic matter along tropical continental margins. *The Science of Nature, 89(1*), 23-30.

Mahta, G., Haile, H., Mahari, F., Mahmud, S., and Beraki, H. (2014). Sea cucumber fisheries in Eritrea (ስ ር ሓት ማግፋፍ ሕድሳ ኣ ብ ኤሪትራ). Unpublished technical report from MMR, Sea Cucumber Fisheries in Eritrea.

Naheed, S. (2015). Threat to biodiversity in the Red Sea along the Eritrean Coast: An overview. *Asian Mirror-International Journal of Research, 2*(1), 21-37.

National Fisheries Corporation of Eritrea(2018). Data provided from the National Fisheries Corporation. Unpublished report.

Richards, J. A., & Jia, X. (2005). *Remote sensing digital image analysis: An introduction* (4th ed). Berlin, Germany: Springer.

Spalding, M., Kainuma, M., & Collins, L. (2010). *World atlas of mangroves* (1st ed.). Earthscan, London.

Wilkie, M. L. & Fortune, S. (2003). Status and trends of mangrove extent area worldwide. Forest Resources Assessment Working Paper No. 63. FAO, Rome.

Yuan, F., Sawaya, K. E, Loeffelholz, B. C., & Bauer, M. E. (2005). Land cover classification and change analysis of the Twin Cities (Minnesota) Metropolitan area by multitemporal

Landsat remote sensing. *Remote Sensing of Environment, 98* (2 & 3), 317-328.

Zekeria, Z. A. (2018). Coastal and marine disasters in the Eritrean Coast of the Red Sea and their mitigation measures. *Journal of Eritrean Studies, 8*(2), 133-164.

Seasonal correlation of changes on SST and Surface Chl-*a* in the Southern Red Sea: based on remote sensing

Hadgu Eyesab Kidanemariam,[1] Zekeria Abdelkerim[2] and Habtom Emru Hagos[3]

Abstract

Tropical water bodies, such as the Red Sea, are among the warmest, most saline, and less fertile water bodies in the world. The Red Sea is a semi-enclosed geographic basin, receives no permanent river discharge and gets less rain fall, and thus evaporation exceeds precipitation. The southern Red Sea and the Eritrean territorial waters remain less studied and the existing literatures provide little information regarding phytoplankton distribution and oceanographic factors influencing primary productivity.

The purpose of the present study is, therefore, to investigate the seasonal and spatial relationship of sea surface temperature (SST) and surface chlorophyll-a (Chl-*a*) concentration; the second goal is to assess SST which is believed to be a proxy of nutrient availability. In this study, satellite data of Chl-*a* and SST are used to explain the seasonal and special variation and relationship of Chl-*a* and SST. The daily surface Chl-*a* data is acquired from ESA–OC-CCI ocean color website and the weekly (8 day) SST are collected from MODIS Aqua from Ocean color website of NASA.

The data is analyzed using R-studio and QGIS. The result indicates that both Chl-*a* and SST show an intense magnitude in the summer unlike what is believed in the tropical waters, that is, both of these parameter are inversely related. This is most likely because, the southern Red Sea

---

[1] Lecturer, Department of Biology, Mai Nefhi College of Science, Eritrea. Email: wedijosiab@gmail.com.
[2] Associate Professor, Department of Biology, Mai Nefhi College of Science, Eritrea. Email: z-a-zekeria@yahoo.com.
[3] Acting Director, Quality Control Laboratory, Ministry of Marine Resources, Eritrea.

water is ventilated by advection (horizontal movement of currents) from the upwelling areas of Gulf of Aden driven by the monsoon winds. This is dissimilar to the tropical waters of its counterpart, which are refreshed by convective overturning (vertical water movement).

Keywords: sea surface temperature (SST); surface chlorophyll-a (Chl-*a*); southern Red Sea; correlation; productivity.

1. Introduction

The Red Sea is the world's northernmost tropical sea, and part of the tropical Indo-Pacific Ocean, with extensive shallow shelves that support 3.8% of the world's coral reefs including many endemic species to the region which occur nowhere else in the world (DiBattista *et al.*, 2015; Sheppard *et al.*, 1992; Sea Around Us, 2007).

The arid nature of the region, hot tropical climate, high levels of solar radiation, high evaporation, high salinity, limited rainfall, absence of permanent rivers, and seasonal variability in monsoon wind direction, create some of the harshest environmental conditions found in the tropics, second only to the Arabian Gulf (Bruckner *et al.*, 2012). These extreme conditions are particularly challenging for marine creatures (Racault *et al.*, 2015). These extreme physical oceanographic conditions control the bio-dynamics and fundamental ecological functions like the phytoplankton productivity.

Sea Surface Temperature (SST) variability basically allows to explore the relationship between the presence of colder waters (which are potentially richer in nutrients) and higher Chl-*a* concentrations (Raitsos *et al.*, 2015; Raitsos *et al.*, 2013; Acker *et al.*, 2008). An important application of SST sensing is identification of sites of upwelling, where rising cold water brings nutrients to the surface from the bottom sea floor. In such sites, phytoplankton and zooplankton growth is enhanced and large concentrations of fish are attracted.

SST is high in the southern Red Sea and generally decreases from south to north, ranging from 31.7°C in the south to 26.0°C in the north (Rushdi, 2015). During summer, the SST is higher (reaches up to 32°C around 14°N), than in winter, in the southern region. However there is lower SST along the Strait of Bab-al-Mendeb due to the influx of cooler water from the Gulf of Aden (Morcos, 1970). In the southern part of the basin the monsoon wind direction noticeably molds SST distribution (Edwards & Head, 1987; Morcos, 1970).

There are two wind patterns controlled by the monsoon system. These are *northwest* which are prevalent in the Summer season from May to September and *southeast* which are dominant in the Winter season from October to April. A combined effect of the temperature, salinity and wind intensity creates a physical barrier in the Red Sea called thermo-haline. This physical barrier acts as a barrier that prevents mixing of the surface and deeper waters. Currents in the Red Sea result largely from winds movement and density gradients in the water column that vary seasonally due to changes in temperature, prevailing winds, and evaporation (Sofianos & Johns 2002; Yao & Hoteit, 2015; Papadopoulos *et al.*, 2015; Yao *et al.*, 2014; Murray & Johns, 1997; Morcos, 1970; Neumann & McGill, 1962).

In the earlier days, it was difficult to investigate large scale oceanographic process. Such studies required collection of large set of data from the field using expensive and labor intensive techniques. However, at present, researchers use remote sensed data to produce promising results to understand the mysterious processes of the ocean (Ackleson, 2003; Robinson, 2010). Therefore remote sensing has become a viable and effective alternative method for studying the large marine ecosystems.

Although studies on the Red Sea oceanography started many years before the 1900s (Ehrenberg, 1838 as sited in Ismael, 2005, p. 567), in recent years satellite-borne sensor measurements for multiple years have been helpful in identifying Red Sea circulation of surface features and estimating average trends in SST and productivity (e.g., Racault *et al.*, 2015; Raitsos *et al.*, 2013; Brewin *et al.*, 2013; Raitsos *et al.*, 2011; Acker *et al.*, 2008).

Acker *et al.*, (2008) investigated the biological dynamics of the northern Red Sea using synoptic view of Chl-*a* and SST from space generated by SeaWiFS. Results from the study showed, lower temperature in the northern part is as a result of convective overturning of water which brings nutrients to the surface and increase the Chl-*a* concentration. This situation results in negative correlation between Chl-*a* and SST at this part of the basin. Recently a number of studies have been conducted to investigate the relationship between productivity and SST. A synoptic observation was made in the Red Sea based on MODIS Aqua, to study Chl-*a* based on SST variations (Raitsos *et al.*, 2013). Most of the reports (e.g., Raitsos *et al.*, 2013; Raitsos *et al.*, 2015; Alkawri & Gamoyo, 2014; Acker *et al.*, 2008), indicate that the southern Red Sea productivity is high during the cold season (winter) than in the hot season (summer). However, other works have showed summer blooms in the southern Red Sea (Shaikh *et al.*, 1986; Dreano *et al.*, 2016; Racault *et al.*, 2015).

There is a controversy between the earlier reports (Acker *et al.*, 2008; Raitsos *et al.*, 2013; Raitsos *et al.*, 2015), that stated the Chl-a and SST are inversely correlated in the Red Sea as in all tropical waters, and the recent findings (Dreano *et al.*, 2016; Racault *et al.*, 2015), that state high productivity aligns with hot climate during summer in the southern Red sea.

This study aims at exploring the seasonality of phytoplankton distribution with respect to temperature and compares the results with earlier studies.

A. Objectives of the study

The general aim of this study is to investigate the correlation between SST and the seasonal patterns of primary productivity in the southern part of the Red Sea, including the Eritrean territory, based on remote sensed data sets. The study also aims at preparing monthly chlorophyll a (Chl-*a)* and SST maps.

B. Significance of the research output

The research output will be a preliminary study of the effect of temperature on the seasonal variability of surface Chl-*a*. SST can be easily retrieved from satellite imagery than Chl-*a*. Therefore if the correlation of SST to primary productivity is investigated then one can easily predict monthly and seasonal Chl-*a* variability. Furthermore this research can help to determine abundance and biodiversity trends of other marine organisms including Pisces. This is because directly or indirectly virtually all marine creatures depend on phytoplankton, the primary producers for food. Thus, the seasonal variability of SST directly influences the productivity of primary producers and indirectly influences the productivity of small pelagic fishes. This research may form a basis for advanced researches such as for refining Maximum Sustainable Yield (MSY) estimates and identifying Potential Fishing Zones (PFZ) to harvest pelagic and other fishes in ecologically and economically sustainable manner in the Eritrean coastal waters of the Red Sea.

The research output can also play a great role in assessing the effect of climate change on the marine environment and the role of the sea as a sink to CO_2. The inconspicuous microscopic marine phytoplankton accounts for only 1-2% of the total global biomass but is responsible for producing 90%- 96% of the ocean surface carbohydrates. They bind at least 50 trillion kilograms of carbon into carbohydrates each year and contribute about 50% of the food made by photosynthesis on the planet. Therefore, this can give an awareness and understanding in ocean acidification and the delicate marine ecosystems, like coral reefs, in the region.

C. Study area

The geographic location of the study area is the southern Red Sea south of 18^0N and north of 12^0N including the coasts of Eritrea, Yemen and Saudi Arabia (Fig. 1). These areas have extensive shallow continental shelve extending up to the middle part of the Red Sea. The depth is shallow about 50% under 100 mts. with sandy bottom. The narrowest (30km maximum width along the Strait of Bab-al-Mendeb) and the widest (355km along the central part of the Eritrean coast, Massawa) part of the Red Sea is found in the study area (Rasul *et al.*, 2015). The southern Red Sea comprises of two large archipelagos: Dahlak and Farasan, which are characterized by extensive coral reefs and mangrove forests.

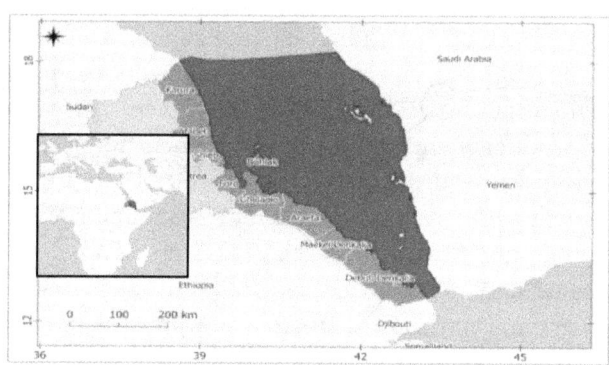

Figure 1. Map showing the study area of the southern Red Sea and the Eritrean coast.

2. Methodology and data sets

A. The Datasets description

i. *Chlorophyll-a*

In this study, the European space agency (ESA) Ocean Color Climate Change Initiatives (OC-CCI) ocean products are utilized. The OC-CCI products are novel products (http://www.esa oceancolour-cci.org, accessed in May 2018). These products are provided by merging four different satellites: (MERIS, MODIS, VIIRS, and SeaWiFS). The output datasets have an advantage of providing better spatial and temporal coverage. These datasets are by far better than using individual sensors (Dreano *et al.*, 2016). Chl-*a* in the OC-CCI products has units of mg m^{-3}. According to the OC-CCI product user guide v3.1, the dataset is created by band-shifting and bias-correcting MERIS, MODIS and VIIRS data to match SeaWiFS data, and computed per-pixel uncertainty estimates. Moreover these data sets are binned together to level 3 (L3) with a spatial resolution of 4 km^2 to have better spatial and temporal resolution, mapped on daily bases.

The data are found in a special format. They are stored as CF-compliant NetCDF as mandated by the ESA CCI Data Standards Working Group. NetCDF is a self-documenting format, meaning that the majority of the information needed to correctly use and interpret the data is incorporated into the file metadata. All files contain CF-compliant latitude, longitude and time dimensions (Grant *et al.*, 2017).

ii. *Sea Surface Temperature (SST)*

SST data were downloaded from MODIS Aqua platform Imaging Spectroradiometer from NASA Ocean color website, http://oceancolor.gsfc.nasa.gov (accessed in May 2018). Data obtained from the website is an average for 8 days for day and night conditions in ^{0}C units and is stored in NetCDF file format. MODIS SST (MOD 28) is acquired in level 3 (L3) in spatial resolution of ≈4km^{2}.

3. Data analysis

This study started in June 2017 and ended in May 2018. The seasonal time windows are defined in this study as summer (June to September), autumn (October to December), winter (January to mid-March) and spring (mid-March to May) similar to what may have been suggested by Raitsos *et al.*, (2013). This study utilizes QGIS and spatial statistical R studio open source softwares.

A. Satellite data imagery visualization and analysis

First both the datasets (Chl-*a* and SST) were downloaded in NetCDF format (.nc) globally. These datasets were opened in R studio by using *ncopen()* under ncdf4 library. All images were rasterized using *raster()* function and after that the data was projected into WGS 84 using *proj4string()* function. Then the data become compatible for overlay with the shapefile of the southern Red Sea with WGS 84 projection and the global data was cropped into the study area of the southern Red Sea using *crop()* function. For Chl-*a* datasets, the daily images of each month were merged together into single image by using *merge()*. A single image was plotted for each month by using *plot()*. Likewise, the SST datasets (in 8-day basis) were merged together (composite) to give monthly average images. The SST images were manipulated using the color Ramp Palette into heat colors:

> *plot(X, col=colorRampPalette(c("blue", "white", "red"))(255))*
> where *X* is the raster SST image.

B. Extraction of data from satellite imagery into a csv table

In order to evaluate the seasonal variation in SST and Chl-a in the study area, the data was extracted from satellite images into Excel sheet. To do this, first the southern Red Sea Shapefile boundary was used. Then, 10,000 random points were generated within the southern Red Sea shapefile in QGIS software. These random points were used to extract values from the satellite imagery for both Chl-*a* and SST in R studio into csv (comma delimited). The random points were added to R studio. Then a tabular data was extracted from the satellite imagery by using a function *extract(x)*.

extract(X, Buffer=1000, Randompoints, fun=mean, df=TRUE)
Where X is the satellite image and Random points are the random points generated

The value of every single point was acquired by creating 1000 mts. buffer or diameter around each point. The extracted tabular data was then exported by calling R to save by the code *write.csv (Z,"Y.csv")* where Z is the extracted value and Y.csv is the name of tabular csv file to be saved. Some of the tabular data in the Excel exhibit null (NA) values then the NA (null) values were easily removed by replacing them automatically with empty cells in Excel.

During the summer months (June to September) there is little satisfactory satellite observation to Chl-*a* and have null values. Therefore fill gap techniques were applied to these images by interpolation.

4. Results and Discussion

A. Seasonal SST Trends

Weakly SST images were downloaded from MODIS aqua ocean color from NASA ocean color web site http://oceancolor.gsfc.nasa.gov (Section 2.A.ii). According to the satellite images provided in Figure 2, Sea Surface temperature was relatively low in winter months (January to March). The temperature started to rise in the spring (April to June) and becomes high in summer (July to October).

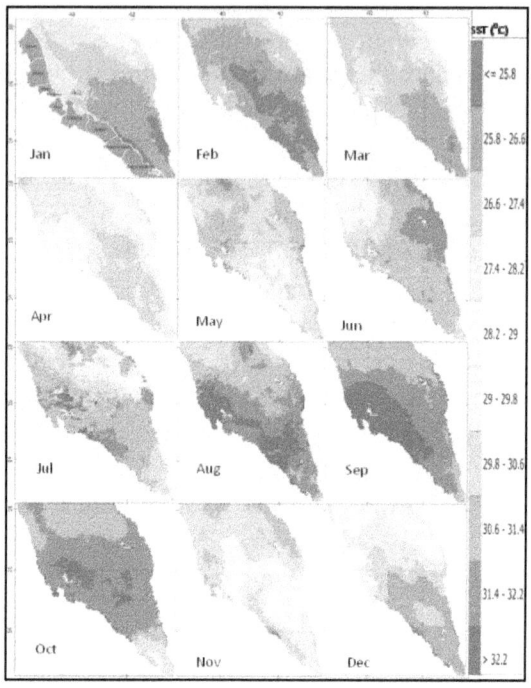

Figure 2. Satellite observation of SST, the bluish color indicates for lower temperature and the reddish color depicts for high SST in the southern Red Sea.

Finally, the temperature values decrease in autumn (October to December). This observation agrees with the findings of Morcos

(1970) and Raitsos *et al.*, (2013). The southern part of the study area showed relatively lower temperature and gradually increased toward the northern part of the study area.

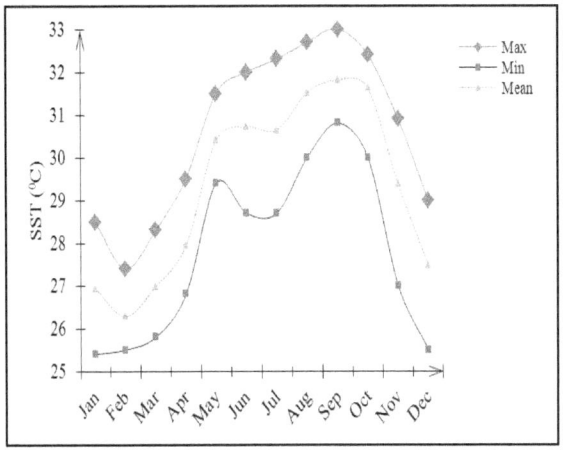

Figure 3. Seasonal variation in SST in the study area. Monthly maximum (diamond), average (triangle) and minimum (square) values are shown.

According to Edwards & Head (1987), the seasonal SST distribution in the southern Red Sea is governed by seasonal monsoon winds reversals. During summer winds blow from north to south and carry colder water from higher latitudes. As the water moves south wards, (lower latitude) its temperature increases. During winter winds reverse their direction and blow north wards and carry colder water from the upwelling area of the Gulf of Aden and the water get hotter as it inters the Red Sea and moves north wards (Dreano *et al.*, 2016; Sofianos & Johns 2003).

The tabular SST data extracted from satellite data shows seasonal variation similar to patterns revealed by the satellite images. As indicated in Fig. 3, SST shows cyclic patterns from high values in summer to low values in winter season. In the summer months the temperature reaches a maximum of 31.8^{0}C and in winter, the lowest temperature of 26.3^{0}C was recorded.

Temperature record from the field around Massawa using HOBO[ware] Temperature loggers during the study period show good compliance with the satellite data with high seasonal variation. Two HOBO[ware] temperature loggers were deployed around Massawa coasts (one in eastern part of Green Island and second in Twalet reef) at 1m depth. The loggers record temperature every 30 min interval automatically. Finally the data that was collected in the data loggers' memory was downloaded and analyzed using the HOBO[ware] pro software. As depicted in figure 4 below, high temperature in summer and lower in winter seasons. However the *in situ* data indicated high range of variation between minimum and maximum (26.2 ^{0}C and 34.9^{0}C). The range is most likely because the area is semi enclosed lagoon and nearest to the land mass. This area does not affected by current and wind agitation.

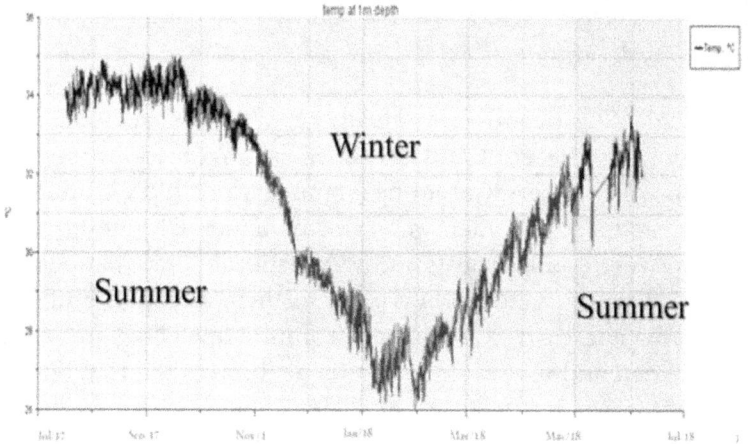

Figure 4. Seasonal variation of temperature around Massawa measured using HOBO[ware] *Temperature loggers.*

B. Surface Chl-*a*

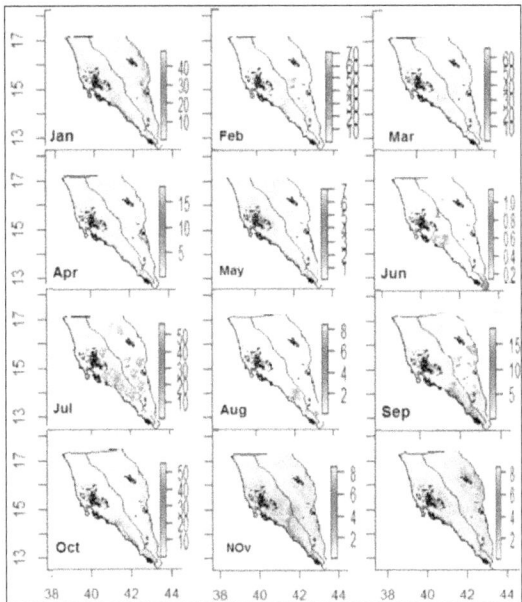

Figure 5. Satellite observation of chlorophyll-a imagery in the southern Red Sea.

The satellite sensor observation on the southern Red Sea shows on the average 2.7μg/L of Surface Chlorphyll-a. During the Summer months the average surface Chl-*a* is higher and the initiation starts in June and reaches maximum in July (≈3.8μg/L), then productivity gradually declines to an average of 2.8 μg/L in autmn; then productivity greatly increases in January reaching upto ≈3.9μg/L and finally gradually declines in the Spring months until May, with an average Chl-*a* of 1.5μg/L (Fig.4). Comperatively the summer and winter months are more productive than the autumn and spring seasons.

The relatively higher summer productivity in the southern Red Sea could be caused by *Northwest* monsoon winds that facilated the entrance of the intermediate layer of nutrient-rich water from the upwelling region in the Gulf of Aden called Gulf of Aden

Intermediate Water (Dreano *et al.*, 2016). The intense productivity in the winter season is mainly governed by the *southeast* monsoon winds which enforces the nutrient rich surface Gulf of Aden water to enter and nourishes the nutrient deficient water of the southern Red Sea. Productivity is high in southern part of the study area than the northern part of the study area. As nutrient rich surface Gulf of Aden water goes north ward the nutrient content of the current gets diminished by the uptake of phytoplankton, as a result the surface Chl-*a* decreases from south to north within the study area as is seen in Figure 4 which is similar to the result of Papadopoulos *et al.*, (2015); Raitsos *et al.*, (2015); Raitsos *et al.*, (2013); and Acker *et al.*, (2008).

C. Correlation between Chl-*a* and SST

The application of SST on productivity studies is employed as a surrogate measure of many environmental parameters such as upwelling, currents, mixed layer depth, photosynthetically active radiation, intensity of Chl-*a*. Therefore finding the measure of SST can characterize a productivity of an area.

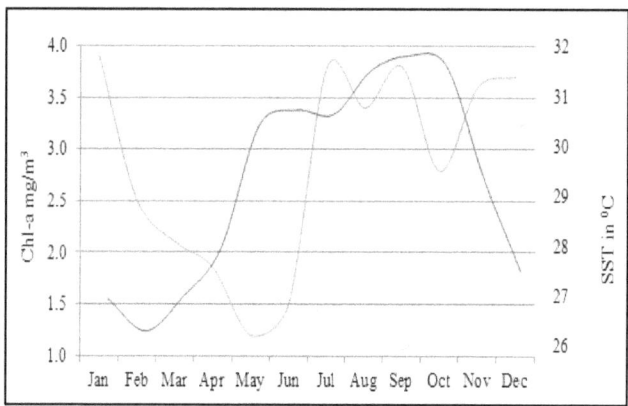

Figure 6. Graph showing the correlation between Chl-a and SST). In the summer months SST and Chl-a have positive correlation and in winter season show negative correlation as SST increases but surface Chl-a decreases.

As a rule of tomb SST and Chl-*a* are inversely correlated. This is because when nutrient rich bottom cold water come up to the photic zone where there is light and thus plants like phytoplankton live, then algal growth boosted hence productivity increases.

In the southern Red Sea temperature and Chl-*a* quantity are inversely correlated during the winter season ($r = -0.67$) and positively correlated in the summer season ($r = 0.84$). During the hot summer season the study area exhibits relatively high productivity. At this time the *northwest* monsoon winds, sails the hot, saline northern surface Red Sea waters from north to south and continue its way out to Gulf of Aden and this results the southern Red Sea surface water to be hotter.

At the same time this area show high productivity due to the entrance of the nutrient loaded Gulf of Aden Intermediate Water (GAIW) below the surface to replace the nutrient deficient hot surface water flow into the Gulf.

The present paradigm in the tropical waters is negative correlation between SST and Chl-*a*. Warm waters are expected to have low productivity due to nutrient deficiencies by stratification (Behrenfeld *et al.*, 2006), and the tropical waters are ventilated by convective vertical overturning processes. As a result, nutrient loaded, deeper and colder water influx to the surface, the SST of the area decreases, and productivity of the environment increases. In this case hot waters are associated with low productive areas. Although the southern Red Sea is expected to have high thermal stratification during the hot season (summer), the unique characteristics of this area causes a positive relationship between SST and Chl-*a*, unlike the tropical waters of its counterpart. This is because, the southern Red Sea depends on wind induced horizontal currents for their nutrient nourishment rather than vertical convective overturning processes (Raitsos *et al.*, 2015).

The horizontal wind movements are significantly strong enough to bring nutrient rich water from the Indian Ocean (Dreano *et al.*, 2016).

5. Conclusions and perspectives

The result presented in the study area along the southern Red Sea provides seasonal variation of surface SST and Chl-*a* based on satellite remote sensing datasets. Accordingly, SST is high in the summer months and gradually decreases in autumn and winter season, and then temperature slowly rises in the spring months. Regarding productivity, there is high productivity during the hot summer and colder winter seasons. During the summer months, the southern Red Sea possesses higher productivity and high temperature, which shows a positive correlation between Chl-*a* and SST. Usually, high thermal stratification is expected during the hot seasons in tropical waters. Consequently the surface water is expected to have low productive. The southern Red Sea is productive at this harsh condition the same as the cold winter season, for it depends on horizontal advection, induced by winds (Dreano *et al.*, 2016; Raitsos *et al.*, 2015). More importantly, this findings show that temperature is not proxy of nutrient availability in this region contrary to Raitsos *et al.* (2013) expectations. Whereas during the cold season there is negative correlation between Chl-*a* and SST.

Therefore, the unique characteristics of the southern Red Sea implies, temperature does not determine the productivity of the southern Red Sea during the hot summer season. And we cannot depend on SST to assess productivity and thus difficult to apply on fisheries managements like prediction of potential fishing zones, estimating fisheries abundance and determining fishing seasons (opening and closing for fishing). But during the cold winter season, the colder surface waters are associated with high productivity and SST studies can be important information on estimate fisheries abundance and potential fishing grounds. Along the western part of the southern Red Sea in the Eritrean coast (Foro, Gelaelo, Areata and the southern part of the Dahlak archipelago coasts), there is low SST measures and high productivity, and accordingly we believe this area is associated with high fish abundance and hence can be delineated as potential fishing grounds. But more studies may be required to investigate if these productive areas are associated with abundant fish availability.

Although these findings are of immediate importance to Eritrea locally, they can give an important insight in the southern Red Sea as a whole for climate change concept, fisheries management plans and for validating ecosystem models that are being developed for the southern Red Sea and its counterpart tropical waters.

Acknowledgement

It had been a difficult job for it requires patience, concentration, technical skill and more importantly reading many articles to accomplish this thesis. I would like to convey my heartfelt gratitude to my advisor, Dr. Zekeria Abdelkerim Zekeria, for his constant guidance, advice and helpful discussion. I especially thank to GIERI project for funding the thesis and Mr. Pekka Hurskainen for his continuous technical support and for downloading satellite data for me.

I owe my deepest gratitude to my beloved children Hadab, Aloniab and Aseniab for their great patience and my wife Engineer Abrehet Solomon for being on my side and always giving me the strength and wisdom to be sincere in my work, for setting high moral standards and supporting me through hard work, and believed that I could do it and for her unselfish love and affection.

References

Ackelson, S. (2003). Light in shallow waters: A brief research review. *Limnology and Oceanography*, *48*(1, part_2), 323-328.

Acker, J., Leptoukh G., Shen S., Zhu T. & Kempler S., (2008). Remotely-sensed chlorophyll a observations of the northern Red Sea indicate seasonal variability and influence of coastal reefs. *Journal of Marine Systems*, *69* (3 & 4), 191-204.

Alkawri, A., & Gamoyo, M. (2014). Remote sensing of phytoplankton distribution in the Red Sea and Gulf of Aden. *Acta Oceanologica Sinca* (English edition), *33*(9), 93-99.

Behrenfeld, M. J., O'Malley R. T., Siegel D. A., McClain C. R., Sarmiento, J. L., Feldman G. C., Milligan A. J., Falkowski P. G., Letelier R. M., & Boss E. S., (2006). Climate-driven trends in contemporary ocean productivity. *Nature*, *444* (7120), 752-755.

Brewin, R. J. W., Raitsos D. E., Dall'Olmo G., Zarokanellos N., Jackson T., Racault M-F, Boss, E. S., Sathyendranath, S., Jones, B. & Hoteit, I. (2015). Regional ocean-color chlorophyll algorithms for the Red Sea. *Remote Sensing of Environment*, *165*, 64-85.

Bruckner, A., Rowlands G., Riegl B., Purkis S., Williams A., & Renaud P. (2012). *Atlas of Saudi Arabian red sea marine habitats*. Khaled bin Sultan Living Oceans Foundation, Landover, MD: Panoramic Press.

Dibattista, J. D., Choat, J. H., Gaither, M. R., Hobbs, J.-P. A., Lozano-Cortés, D. F., Myers, R. F., Paulay, G., Rocha, L. A., Toonen, R. J., Westneat, M. W., & Berumen, M. L. (2015). On the origin of endemic species in the Red Sea. *Journal of Biogeography*, *43*(1), 13-30.

Dreano, D., Raitsos D.E., Gittings J., Krokos G., Hoteit I. (2016). The Gulf of Aden intermediate water intrusion regulates the southern red sea summer phytoplankton blooms. *PLoS ONE* *11*(12), 1-20.

Edwards A. J. & Head, S. M. (eds.), *Key environments: Red Sea*. Oxford: Pergamon Press.

Grant, M., Jackson T., Chuprin A., Sathyendranath S., Zühlke M., Dingle J., Storm T., Boettcher M., Fomferra N. (2017). Ocean Colour Climate Change Initiative (OC_CCI) – Phase Two, product user guide v3.1. Full information is available at, https://dap.ceda.ac.uk/neodc/esacci/ocean_colour/docs/OC-CCI-PUG-v3.1.pdf.

Ismael, A. A. (2015). Phytoplankton of the Red Sea. In Rasul, N. M. A. & Stewart, I. C. F. (eds.), *The Red Sea* (pp. 567-83). Berlin, Heidelberg: Springer-Verlag.

Morcos, S. M. (1970). Physical and chemical oceanography of the Red Sea. *Oceanography and Marine Biology, An Annual Review, 8* 73-202.

Murray, S. P., & Johns W. (1997). Direct observations of seasonal exchange through the Bab el Mandeb Strait. *Geophysical Research Letters, 24*(21), 2557-2560.

Neumann, A. C. & McGill, D. A. (1962). Circulation of the Red Sea in early summer. *Deep Sea Research, 8* (3 & 4), 223-235.

Papadopoulos, V. P., Zhan, P., Sofianos, S., Raitsos E., Qurban, M., Abualnaja, Y., Bower, A., Kontoyiannis, H., Pavlidou, A. S., Asharaf, M., Zarokanellos, N., & Hoteit, I. (2015). Factors governing the deep ventilation of the Red Sea. *Journal of Geophysical Research, 120*(11), 7493-7505.

Racault, M-F, Raitsos, D. E., Berumen, M. L., Brewin, R. J. W., Platt, T., Sathyendranath, S., & Hoteit, I. (2015). Phytoplankton phenology indices in coral reef ecosystems: Application to ocean-color observations in the Red Sea. *Remote Sensing of Environment, 160*, 222-234.

Raitsos, D. E., Hoteit, I., Prihartato, P. K., Chronis, T., Triantafyllou, G., Abualnaja ,Y. (2011). Abrupt warming of the Red Sea. *Geophysical Research Letters, 38*(14), 1-5.

Raitsos, D. E., Pradhan, Y., Brewin, R. J. W., Stenchikov, G., & Hoteit, I. (2013). Remote sensing the phytoplankton Seasonal Succession of the Red Sea. *PLoS ONE, 8*(6), 1-9.

Raitsos, D. E., Yi, X., Platt, T., Racault, M-F, Brewin, R. J. W., Pradhan, Y., Papadopoulos, V., Sathyendranath, S., & Hoteit, I. (2015). Monsoon oscillations regulate fertility of the Red Sea. *Geophysical Research Letters*, *42*(3), 855-862.

Robinson, I. S. (2010). *Understanding the oceans from space: The unique applications of satellite oceanography*. Berlin, Heidelberg: Springer-Verlag.

Rushdi, A. I. (2015). Calcite and aragonite saturation states of the Red Sea and biogeochemical impacts of excess carbon dioxide. In Rasul, N. M. A. & Stewart, I. C. F. (eds.). *The Red Sea* (pp. 267-279). Berlin, Heidelberg: Springer-Verlag.

Sea Around Us (2007). A global database on marine fisheries and ecosystems. Fisheries Center, University of British Columbia, Vancouver, Canada.

Shaikh, E. A., Roff, J. C. & Dowidar, N. M. (1986). Phytoplankton ecology and production in the Red Sea off Jiddah, Saudi Arabia. *Marine Biology*, *92*(3), 405-416.

Sheppard, C. J. R., Price A., & Roberts C. (1992). *Marine ecology of the Arabian region: patterns and processes in extreme tropical environments* (1st ed.). London: Academic Press.

Sofianos, S. S., & Johns, W. E. (2002). An Oceanic General Circulation Model (OGCM) investigation of the Red Sea circulation: 1. Exchange between the Red Sea and the Indian Ocean. *Journal of Geophysical Research*, *107* (C11), 3196-3207.

Yao, F., & Hoteit, I. (2015). Thermocline regulated seasonal evolution of surface chlorophyll in the Gulf of Aden. *PLoS ONE*, *10*(1), 1-11.

Yao, F., Hoteit, I., Pratt, L. J., Bower, A. S., Zhai, P., & Köhl, A. (2014). Seasonal overturning circulation in the Red Sea: 1. Model validation and summer circulation. *Journal of Geophysical Research: Oceans*. 119: 2238-2262.

A Geospatial Approach to Malaria Risk Analysis in Ne'us Zoba Ghindae, Eritrea

Hammid Mohammed Ibrahim[1] and Md. Minhajul Hoda[2]

Abstract

The landscape of Ne'us Zoba Ghindae, Eritrea, which is dominated by low altitude and moist conditions, creates a favorable environment for mosquito breeding and malaria transmission. A good knowledge and understanding of mosquito ecology, malaria epidemiology, and putative malaria risk factors is imperative for designing effective malaria control measures. In this study, geospatial data and technologies are employed to identify high malaria risk localities in the study area by establishing the relationship among various climatic, topographic and drainage factors. Malaria vector-based risk factors such as temperature, rainfall, altitude, topographic slope, and distance from streams were used to map malaria-hazard areas. Thereafter, the hazard factor map together with the vulnerability factor map (distance from health facilities), and Element at Risk factor maps, were used to generate the final malaria Risk Map. The factor maps were combined using Weighted Multi-Criteria Evaluation (MCE) on QGIS 2.14 platform. The resulting malaria hazard map showed that, 27.9%, 59.9%, 14% and 4.7% of Ne'us Zoba Ghindae are under very high, high, moderate and low malaria hazard levels respectively. The weighted-MCE-based malaria risk map produced from the overlay analysis showed that, 43.5%, 26.5%, 22.3% and 7.8% of the Ne'us Zoba is exposed to very high, high, moderate and low risk respectively. The Weighted MCE-based malaria risk map to the larger part coincided with the reality in ground. Spatial-interpolation of settlement-based malaria cases was also employed to generate a continuous layer of data, for risk map validation. The study demonstrated that, the support of satellite data and the integration of various parameters in GIS help in delineating high risk

---

[1] Lecturer, Department of Geography, College of Business and Social Sciences, Eritrea. Email: hamidmehammed89@gmail.com.
[2] Assistant Professor, Department of Geography, College of Business and Social Sciences, Eritrea. Email: minhajulhoda@rediffmail.com.

areas to inform policy formulations and the design of malaria control/prevention measures.

Keywords: Eritrea; Ne'us Zoba Ghindae; malaria; geospatial; GIS; QGIS; Weighted Multi-Malaria Evaluation (MCE); spatial interpolation.

1. Introduction

Eritrea lies at the northern limit of malaria transmission in Sub-Saharan Africa (Craig *et al.*, 1999), with lengthy dry season, which can limit the intensity of malaria transmission (Graves, 2004). However, the physical diversity of the country creates suitable breeding grounds for mosquitoes in certain regions and seasons, which complicates malaria transmission pattern (Graves, 2004). Moreover, anthropogenic determinants, such as farming activities, construction of water reservoirs and different kind of land use patterns, introduction of irrigation schemes, traditional mining projects, and movement of non-immune people to the endemic malarious areas may worsen the malaria situation in Eritrea (Berhane *et al.*, 2015). The fact that, approximately 70 % of the population resides in malaria-endemic or epidemic areas, in almost two-third of the landmass (Berhane *et al.*, 2015), where the disease is seasonal, highly focal, and unstable, puts Eritrea in a disadvantageous position in terms of malaria control (Nyarango *et al.*, 2006). Specifically, the four endemic Zobas (Gash Barka, Anseba, Semenawi Keyih Bahri and Debub), are characterized by an environment, which is conducive to interactions between the Anopheles mosquito, malaria parasites and human hosts, as well as housing of generally poor quality, which offers little protection from mosquito-human contact (Nyarango *et al.*, 2006).

Eritrea has made considerable progress in reducing malaria prevalence, through a combination of case management, larval habitat management (LHM), wide-scale free distribution of insecticide-treated nets (ITNs), and indoor residual spraying (IRS) in high-prevalence areas (Nyarango *et al.*, 2006). Furthermore, there is generally low nationwide *Plasmodium falciparum* prevalence (Mushinzimana *et al.*, 2006, Berhane *et al.*, 2015). However, according to World Malaria Report (2017), national malaria cases were about 55,995 in 2013; it increased to 66,493 in 2014, then decreased to about 43,682 in 2015. In 2016, the national case load showed sharp increment reaching 71,306 cases, partly due to the high rainfall received in most regions (Ministry of Health, 2016). Moreover, it is reported that, malaria in Eritrea is prone to epidemics, with some perennial transmission along rivers, valleys, dams, as well as irrigation projects (Mushinzimana *et al.*, 2006). The National Malaria Control Program of Eritrea has developed a National Malaria strategic plan to eliminate malaria in Eritrea by 2030 (Ministry of Health, 2016). Interestingly, Malaria elimination has been a priority in the Millennium Development Goals (MDGs), and since then has continued to be central to the Sustainable Development Goals (SDGs), supporting Eritrea's malaria elimination commitments (Ministry of Health, 2016).

In Eritrea, studies about malaria targeted particularly control policies and programs (Keating *et al.*, 2011; Yukich *et al.*, 2009), household risk factor analysis (Sintasath *et al.*, 2005; Berhane *et al.*, 2015), and anti-malarial drug resistance (Berhane, 2017). Generally viewed, despite few research efforts to describe the distribution of malaria vectors (Shililu *et al.*, 2003) and their behavior (Shililu *et al.*, 2004), extensive information regarding the epidemiology of malaria in Eritrea, especially at site-specific level, has been missing or is very limited. In the study area (Ne'us Zoba Ghindae), few researches were conducted in relation to malaria (Habtai *et al.*, 2008; Mohammed *et al.*, 2018). In spite of the public health impact of malaria currently, and malaria resurgence since 2014 in the study area, there is a gap in research on the geo-environmental analysis of malaria. Therefore, there is urgent need to develop dynamic and area-specific risk maps of the study site to identify locations and populations at highest risk. This in turn, will assist for appropriate implementation of targeted preventive measures against malaria.

The development of malaria in an area is highly affected by climatic and topographic factors, like rainfall, temperature, altitude, and topographic slope. GIS and remote sensing can be used to associate such variables with the distribution of mosquito responsible for malaria transmission. Other factors like population density, land-use/cover and proximity to different malaria causing or preventing factors (distance to breeding sites or health facilities) can be also associated with the effect they have on malaria prevalence using the same tools. Therefore, GIS and remote sensing are the appropriate tools to aid malaria control and prevention system through assessing potential malaria risk level of an area. Thus, this study focuses on using GIS and low-resolution satellite imageries (Land sat 8 images and DEM, with 30 mts. resolution and some ancillary data) to generate malaria risk map, using Weighted Multi-Criteria Decision approach for Ne'us Zoba Ghindae.

2. The study area

Ne'us Zoba Ghindae is located at 15^0 20' N and 39^0 15'E and its area is 2026.56 Km^2. The Ne'us Zoba comprises of 13 administrative localities, with several villages dispersed in vast areas. The total population was about 58,200 in 2017. The study area is primarily rural, where the main economic activities of the people are pastoralism, farming and trade. The elevation of the Ne'us Zoba ranges between 118 and 2048 mts. with wide-range temperature situations and bimodal rainfall pattern, resulting in two malaria-transmission seasons, January to March in the low-lying areas and September to November in the highland parts of the Ne'us Zoba. About 58% of the Ne'us Zoba's area gets annual rainfall between 600 to 870 mm. Spatially, the highland north-west parts receive higher rains compared to other parts of the Ne'us Zoba. Temperatures range between 17.9°C and 28.3°C on average, with the hottest days occurring in August, and coldest in January.

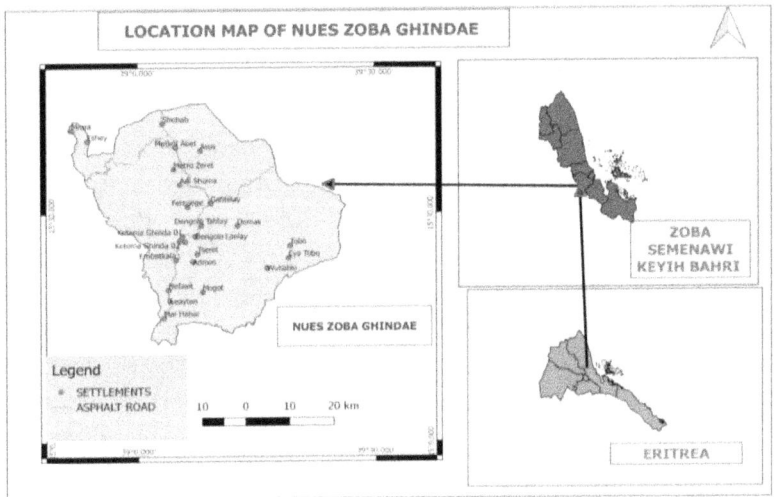

Figure 8. Location map of Ne'us Zoba Ghindae.

3. Materials and methods

A. Data collection

Satellite climate data (Africlim), which is freely available, was used for obtaining Mean Annual Temperature and Precipitation data for the study area. Digital Elevation Model (DEM) of 30m resolution was used to characterize topography of the study area. Moreover, Landsat 8 image of the study area was used for classification of the study area into a number of land use and land cover classes. Vector datasets of streams and medical facilities were acquired from Eritrean Mapping and Information Center (EMIC).

B. Software used

A spatial Multi-Criteria Decision Analysis (MCDA) incorporated into GIS is the method adopted for malaria risk mapping using QGIS 2.14 software.

C. Malaria risk factors /variables investigated

It is reviewed by several studies such as Craig *et al.* (1999) & Tanser *et al.* (2003) that climatic factors (rainfall and temperature) have serious impact on malaria occurrence. Rainfall and temperature are the climatic factors that affect the breeding of the malaria vector. Moreover, altitude is generally considered to play an important role in limiting malaria in the tropical highlands by negatively influencing the breeding of vector species (De Silva & Marshall, 2012). Areas at a high altitude have low transmission when compared to areas at low altitude. Topographic slope is a measurement of how steep or gentle the ground surface is in terms of terrain orientation and is a derivative of DEM.

Interestingly, terrain slope is used as a pivotal factor of water stagnation. It is the measurement of the rate-change of the land per unit distance which may affect the stability of the aquatic habitat (Munga, 2006). Malaria risk is negatively associated with topographic slope, where breeding sites of mosquitos are more likely to be in gentle slopes and plains (Balls *et al.*, 2004). Moreover, presence of health institutions in a particular area is very important for treatment of patients, awareness creation and implementation of preventive measures (Meron, 2010). In connection with this, absence or distant placed health institutions result in difficulties in accessibility and enhanced cost of treatment. These, in turn, influence the prevalence of disease in the locality.

4. Development of malaria hazard, vulnerability and element at risk factor maps

There are three components used in the *Shook* Risk model (Malaria Hazard, Malaria Vulnerability, and Element at Risk) for malaria risk mapping and modelling.

A. Malaria hazard

As a hazard, malaria occurrence is mapped by depending on some of the environmental factors, which contribute to the survival of Anopheles mosquitoes. The malaria incidence and transmission requires an environment with lower elevation (higher temperature), abundance of wet lands, occurrence of gentle slopes, availability of still waters around rivers, and areas of lower drainage density (Negasi, 2008).

B. Malaria vulnerability

It is the susceptibility to be affected by its causal agent (plasmodium *sp.*). Malaria vulnerability analysis and mapping is done based on socio-economic-demographic attributes of the affected human population. WHO (2013) suggested that malaria occurrences is high in communities characterized by low access to health care facilities and low income. The people that live far from health care facilities were identified the most vulnerable to malaria in most Sub-Saharan African countries (Stratton, 2008).

C. Element at risk map

The most facilitating land use and landcover class type for mosquito breeding is considered as *"Element at Risk"*, and is mapped to identify the landuse/cover classes, which deem the highest level of risk for malaria to occur. Mostly swampy areas, irrigated land areas with high vegetation density and built up areas are characterized as land use and landcover classes with high risk of malaria.

Malaria risk is broadly considered as an array of factors that relate to the presence and density of malaria vectors and parasites. A large number of malaria causing factors, including proximity to vector breeding site, inadequate use of control measures and land use plays a big role (Stratton, 2008). Thus, for malaria risk mapping, all hazard, vulnerability and landuse/landcover patterns need to be considered.

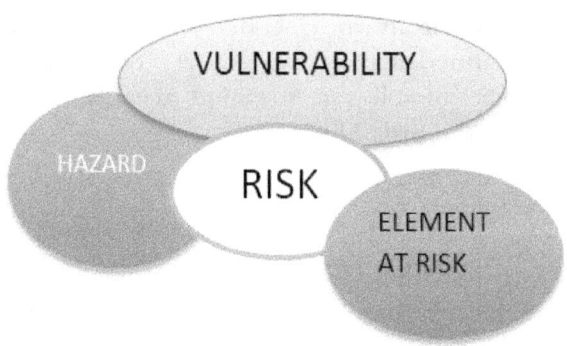

Figure 9. Malaria risk model components.

For the purpose of identifying areas of malaria hazard, seven parameters associated with the environment, including topography, climate and drainage are chosen based on their association with malaria and its vectors. These include factors related to thermal and altitudinal limits, for malaria parasites and vectors; and availability of vector breeding sites (wetlands, precipitation). In addition, Habitat modifying factors, such as slope are also involved in hazard mapping. Moreover, diseases vulnerability components, such as access/distance to health facilities also considered to generate the final malaria risk map.

i. Elevation

Elevation of the study area was reclassified based on the extent of malaria prevalence at different altitudes in accordance to Hanafi-Bojd *et al.* (2012), using the Natural Jenks classification in QGIS platform into four classes, and new values were assigned to each class, as shown on Table 1.

ii. Topographic slope

The slope of the study area was extracted from the DEM and then reclassified into four classes, using the natural-break standard reclassification technique in QGIS environment, considering Zewga (2016) approach of slope-malaria risk association. In the study area, the minimum slope angle along flat sections is $0.7°$, while the maximum slope observed on nearly vertical cliffs is $39°$. A slope category map of Ne'us Zoba Ghindae is prepared for four categories: gentle, moderately steep, steep, and escarpment/cliff (see Figure 1).

iii. Temperature

Temperature raster datasets from *AFRIclim* for Nu`esZoba Ghindae were extracted, where the minimum is $17.9°C$, while the maximum is $28.3°C$. In this study, as in most literatures reviewed, and following mainly Bi *et al.* (2003), average temperature below $21°C$ is considered inappropriate for malaria transmission (lowest hazard level) , while a temperature range of $23°C$ to $30°C$ is deemed conducive for stable transmission.

iv. Rainfall

Raster datasets of mean annual rainfall of the study site were extracted from *AFRIclim*, with range of 265 to 871mm. To determine rainfall-convenience scenario for malaria, Chikodzi

(2013) approach of rainfall hazard level classification was adopted. Places are considered as High malaria hazard categories if annual rainfall is between 600mm-700mm. In addition, places with mean annual rainfall greater than 700mm are considered very high risk areas.

v. Distance to streams

To delineate malaria hazard areas, streams shapefile of the study area were rasterized in GRASS 7.05 software environment. Furthermore, proximity to Streams is measured using the Euclidean distance tool in QGIS 2.14 platform, and buffer zones of river distance created in accordance with Ahmad *et al.* (2017).

vi. Distance from health facilities factor map

The Health facilities shapefile of the study area was rasterized using SAGA rasterization tool to determine the sphere of influence of each health facility, using Euclidean distance. This was done by calculating distance from each health center, and by reclassifying the distances into four classes based on the lowest easily accessible distance, following WHO standards and Zewga (2016).

vii. The element at risk layer

Land use and land cover layer was developed, by reclassifying Landuse and Landcover (LULC) image-file on the basis of malaria susceptibility of each LULC image classes, using supervised classification technique in QGIS 2.14, and verified by ground truth data collected for each land use-land cover types by field survey.

The following chart shows the overall process of malaria risk mapping employed in the research.

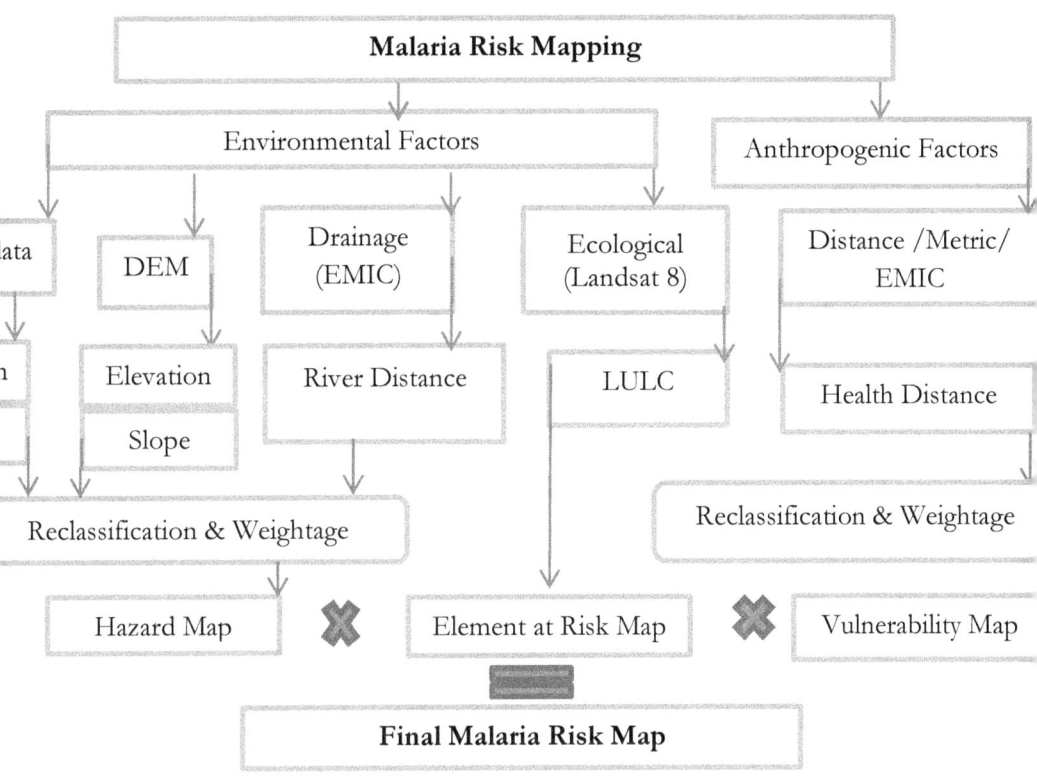

Figure 10. Malaria risk mapping, flowchart.

5. Results

A. Generation of malaria hazard map

Malaria incidence and transmission requires an environment with lower elevation (higher temperature), abundance of wet lands, occurrence of gentle slopes, availability of still waters around rivers, and areas of lower drainage density (Kaya *et al.*, 2002; Negasi, 2008). Thus in this study, it is by overlaying these factors that areas hazardous to malaria were identified. Interestingly, the weights assigned for the hazard components depend more on extensive literature review and expert opinion. The spatial model constructed for the overlay of the factors and creation of the malaria hazard map is given below. Interestingly, Weighted Overlay method assumes that, more favorable factors result in the higher values in the output raster, therefore, identifying these locations as being most at risk.

Equation 1:
Malaria Hazard = 0.25* [Elevation] + 0.10 * [Slope] + 0.30* [Temperature] + 0.20* [Rainfall] + 0.15 * [Stream distance]

Factor	Reclassified Value	Hazard Level & score	Weight
Elevation (mts.)	>2000	Low(1)	0.25
	1200-2000	Moderate(2)	
	800-1200	High(3)	
	<800	Very High(4)	
Slope angle (degree)	> 30	Low(1)	0.10
	15-30	Moderate(2)	
	8-15	High(3)	
	0-8	Very High(4)	
Temperature (°C)	< 21	Low(1)	0.30
	21-23	Moderate(2)	
	23 -25	High(3)	
	25-30	Very High(4)	
Rainfall (mm)	<450	Low(1)	0.20
	450-600	Moderate(2)	
	600-700	High(3)	
	>700	Very High(4)	
Stream Distance (Mts.)	>750	Low(1)	0.15
	500-750	Moderate(2)	
	250-500	High(3)	
	< 250	Very High(4)	

Table 8. Reclassified climate, topography and drainage related hazard factors.

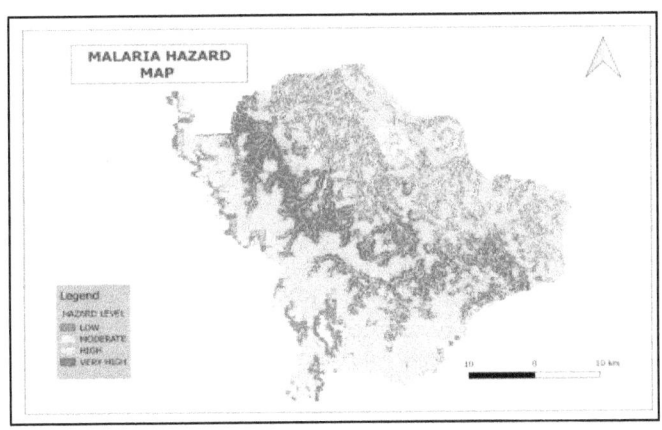

Figure 4. Hazard factor maps.

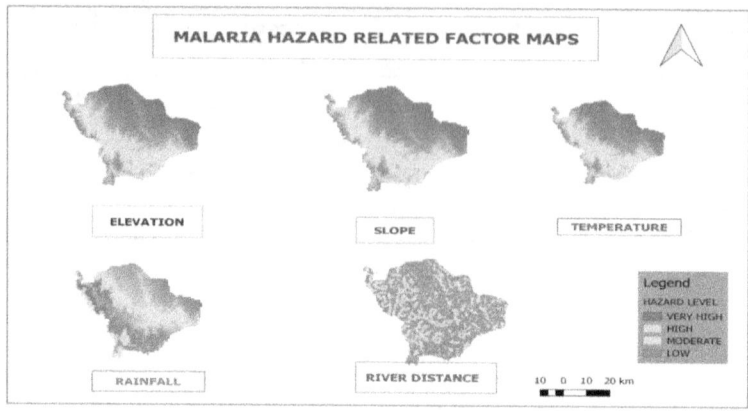

Figure 5. Malaria hazard map.

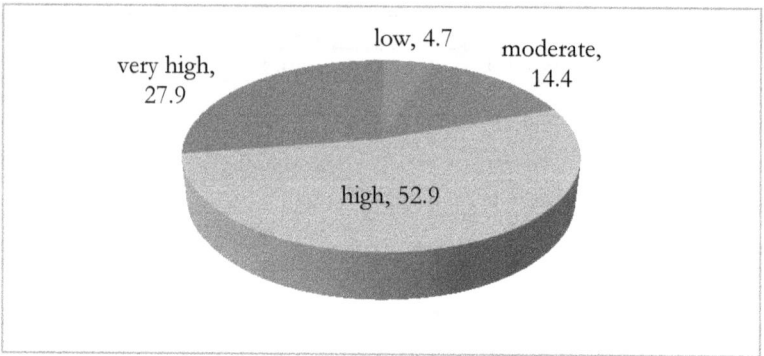

Figure 6. Malaria hazard level areal coverage (in%).

The Malaria hazard map in Figure 5 illustrates that about 566 Sq. Km and 1068 Sq. Km, representing respectively 27.9 percent and 52.9 percent of the total area of the study area is subject to very high and high level of malaria susceptibility. Interestingly, about 14 percent of the study area falls under moderate malaria hazard score. Hence, it is possible to conclude that over 80 percent of the total area is highly exposed to mosquito breeding, and in turn malaria infection, since it is in high and very high malaria hazard score levels. Likewise, the remaining area is either moderately hazardous or with low level of malaria exposure.

The temperature suitability is ideal condition for mosquito proliferation and malaria in turn, associated mainly with the low-elevated landform of the study site. Moreover, significant portion of the study area is nearly level to gentle slope, which affects the drainage system. This may result in the availability of stagnant surface water and the creation of swampy areas, which is a favorable breeding pool for the mosquito vectors. Specifically, nearness of some settlements to rivers and streams could be a risk factor of malaria. In nutshell, the hazard factors of malaria in Ne'us Zoba Ghindae are enormous, in combination with vulnerability factors and the land use and cover type facilitating malaria transmission.

B. Generation of malaria vulnerability map

In assessing the area in urgent need of attention to fight against Malaria, hazard mapping which is based solely on natural conditions, is not sufficient; it also requires the inclusion and consideration of socio-economic/vulnerability factors. In this research, one vulnerability related risk factor (distance to medical facility) is considered, to come up with the malaria vulnerability map, as depicted in Figure 7. WHO (2003) states that areas found within 3 km radius from health centers, are assumed to be at lesser malaria risk than areas found outside this distance. Hence, classes of distances, <3000 mts., 3000-5000 mts., 5000-7000 mts. and >7000 mts. were designated. Accordingly, the classes are labeled as low, moderate, high and very high malaria risks respectively. It can be visually interpreted that the vulnerability of malaria is less in areas close to health institutions (Figure 7).

Factor	Reclassified Value	Hazard Level & score
Vulnerability (Distance from Health Facilities (KM)	<3	Low(1)
	3-5	Moderate(2)
	5-7	High(3)
	>7	Very High(4)

Table 9. Reclassified vulnerability related malaria factor map.

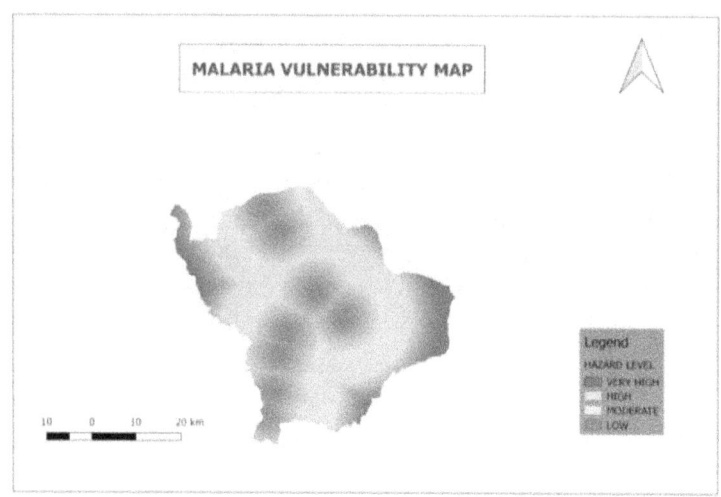

Figure 7. Malaria vulnerability map.

C. Generation of landuse and landcover map

Although identification and visualization of wet and swampy areas, which could be mosquito breeding sites, was difficult due to large areal size of the Ne'us Zoba under consideration, the LULC layer was classified into malaria-relevant classes, including large-scale agriculture, grassland and forest. Overall, three broad land use classes were used. Landcover class of mosaic vegetation and grasslands are considered high and moderate risk sites for malaria, respectively. Places of rain-fed croplands, and irrigational farms were considered as very high risk category. Moreover, urban settlements and densely vegetated areas also constitute very high risk level, while areas of barren land were designated low risk. Interestingly, the study area is dominantly covered by bare-land (non-vegetated, uncultivated farmland and open space) covering a total of about 62 percent. This is followed by mosaic of vegetated areas and grasslands, which accounts for one-fourth of the area and built up, irrigation and rain-fed area, and dense vegetation making for the remaining area (about 11% area).

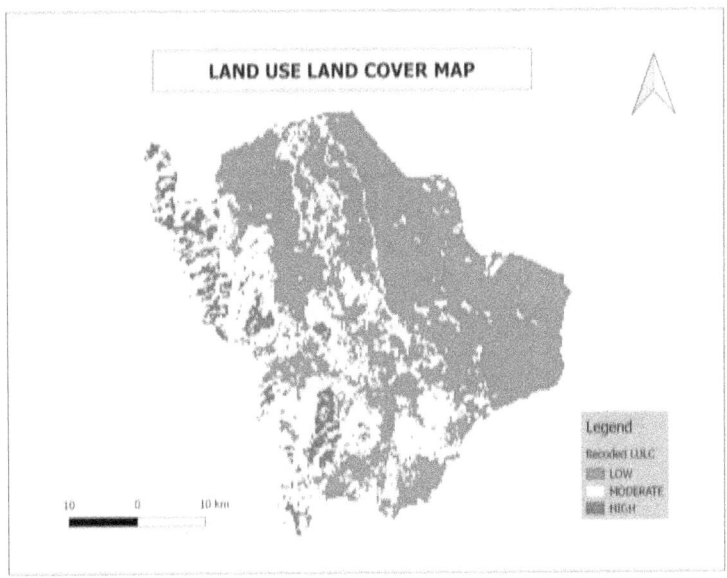

Figure 8. Reclassified Land use and Land cover based malaria risk level.

Factor	Reclassified value	Hazard score	Area coverage (Sq. Km)	(%)
LULC (feature type)	bare lands, sparse vegetation	low	1254.4	62.1
	grasslands, mosaic vegetation	moderate	535.8	26.5
	built up, irrigation & rain-fed area, dense vegetation	high	230.5	11.4

Table 10. Element at Risk malaria risk scores and areal coverage.

D. Overlay analysis and generating malaria risk map

The three components of malaria risk analysis are hazard, element at risk and vulnerability map layers. Thus, the malaria hazard map, vulnerability, and land use land cover map were multiplied to generate the malaria risk indicator map, which is shown in Figure 9. As hazard component is very significant composing the ecologic, topographic, climatic, and drainage factors for malaria transmission, 0.60 (60%) weight was assigned. For element at risk and vulnerability component, 15% and 25% weight were allocated respectively. Moreover, the basis for the calculation of the risk map was the risk computation model, developed by Shook (1997).

According to Shook,

*Equation 2: Risk = Hazard * Element at risk * vulnerability*
Malaria risk = 0.60×[Malaria hazard level]+0.15× [Landuse/cover] +0.25× [Malaria vulnerability]

E. Identified areas of malaria risk

Defining the precise edges of distribution of malaria is difficult, owing to small-scale ecological variability of transmission risk. In reality, there is a gradual, ill-defined transition from perennial-to-seasonal-to-epidemic to malaria-free regions, as well as, from high to low transmission intensity. Malaria transmission is not definable in space, because the edge of distribution is indistinct.

Generally, the produced malaria risk map revealed that major proportions of Ne'us Zoba Ghindae land surface has high to very high-risk, in areas which are characterized generally by a relatively low altitude, gentle slopes, high relative humidity and heavy rains. Interestingly, according to the malaria Risk map and as summarized in Table 4, it is estimated that, about three-fourth of the study area is subjected to very high and high malaria riskiness. Likewise, more than one-fourth of the study area is classified as moderately to low risk in terms of malaria contagion. This quantification of risk areas is done empirically, based on the geo-environmental inputs and proximity factors such as road and medical services distances to malaria hosts. Thus, for analytical convenience, the result obtained was classified into four malaria hotspot ratings.

i. Very high risk areas

Visual interpretation of the generated Malaria Risk Map reveals that, significant portion of Green Belt of Eritrea, as part of Ne'us Zoba Ghindae is the riskiest in the generated malaria risk map, though it has almost no-human settlement. It is mapped so since it has much rainfall (high wetness), dense forests, with low accessibility to roads and health facilities. Thus, these localities are mapped out as part of the potentially suitable areas for mosquito proliferation, though they are without settlement, which reduces its malaria burden.

ii. High risk areas

This zone is characterized by a lot of perennial streams, gentle slope and moderate to low elevation, which provide most conducive environment for the growth of malaria parasite. As displayed in the generated malaria risk map, the high malaria hazard score is scattered in significant portion of the Ne'us Zoba, especially in North central and eastern sections and some portion of southeast of the Ne'us Zoba.

iii. Medium risk areas

These areas are found adjacent to the low risk level, with moderate wetness, high to moderate rainfall and few streams, high to moderate slope and moderate to high elevation. Settlements such as Emabatkala and Mogot lie in the moderate malaria risk areas.

iv. Low risk areas

These areas are considered generally as low priority areas, and characterized by somewhat few settlements, covered with open forest to non- forest, medium rainfall, high slope and high elevation which provides less favorable condition for the malaria parasite to grow. The western part of the Ne'us Zoba with the highland fringe setting is of low risk. This implies that almost all of the elevated areas except the forest-belt of Semenawi Bahri are classified as low malaria risk area.

No.	Rating	Area in Sq. Km	% (area)
1	Low	158.0	7.8
2	Moderate	451.8	22.3
3	High	534.9	26.4
4	Very High	881.3	43.5
Total		2026	100%

Table 11. Reclassified risk map & areal coverage.

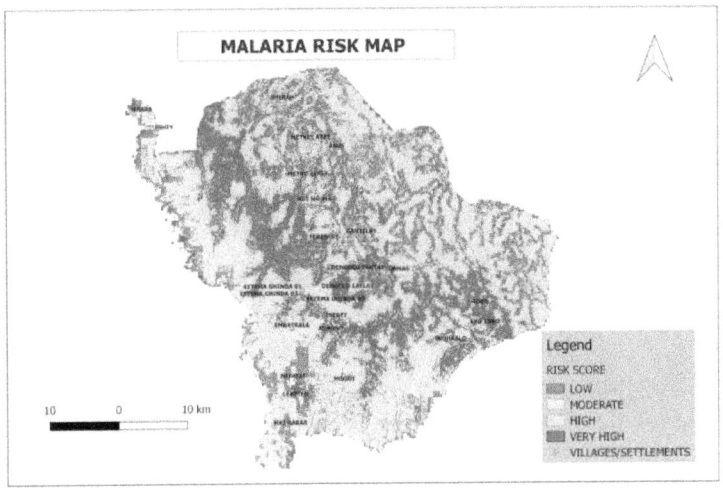

Figure 9. Final malaria risk map.

F. Validation of malaria risk map

In this study, Choloropleth mapping and *Inverse Distance Weighed Interpolation* (IDWI) were employed for the verification of the generated final malaria risk map. The produced malaria risk map is validated using geo-referenced data representing actual reported village level malaria cases of the Ne'us Zoba, covering the period from January 2016 to December 2017. Generally viewed, significant portions of the human settlements of Ne'us Zoba Ghindae fall in the high risk areas of the produced map (see figures 10 and 11).

According to reports from malaria control program of Zoba Semenawi Keih Bahri, prevalence of malaria is higher in the Ne'us Zoba, as compared with the overall data for the country. For instance, the mean national malaria crude prevalence of Eritrea for the year 2017 was estimated to be 12 persons/1000, while that of Ne'us Zoba Ghindae was about 80 persons/1000, which was more than six times. More importantly, in recent years, Ne'us Zoba Ghindae has the highest record of clinical malaria prevalence from the ten Ne'us Zobas of Zoba Semenawi Keih Bahri.

A recent study by Meron *et al.* (2018), and an earlier study by Ceccato *et al.* (2007) on malaria stratification based on malaria health-facility data of 2012 to 2016 and 1998 to 2003 in Eritrea categorized Ne'us Zoba Ghindae into highest and Moderate-Incidence clusters respectively. Moreover, according to the 2016 Ministry of Health's Health Management and Information System (HMIS) report, Ne'us Zoba Ghindae ranked second in terms of malaria incidence with about 11,302 per 100,000 populations.

Overall, malaria showed an increasing trend in the study site during the last five-year period from 2013 to 2017. The prevalence has shown sharp rise from 2013 to 2014, almost five-fold, very high increment from 2015 (1,744 cases) until it reached its peak in 2016 at about 7,163 cases, yielding a crude prevalence of 13.8% and accounting for nearly 10% from of the national malaria case load burden for that year. Compared to previous years, the malaria peak year received an unusually higher amount of rain, during December 2015 and January 2016. Malaria prevalence dropped to nearly greater than half (4, 249 cases, with an annual parasite incidence [API] of 82/1000 population) in the year 2017.

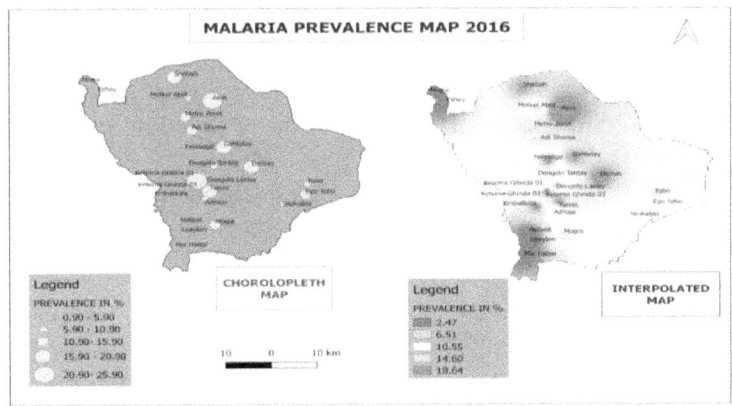

Figure 10. Malaria prevalence map and its interpolated form, 2016.

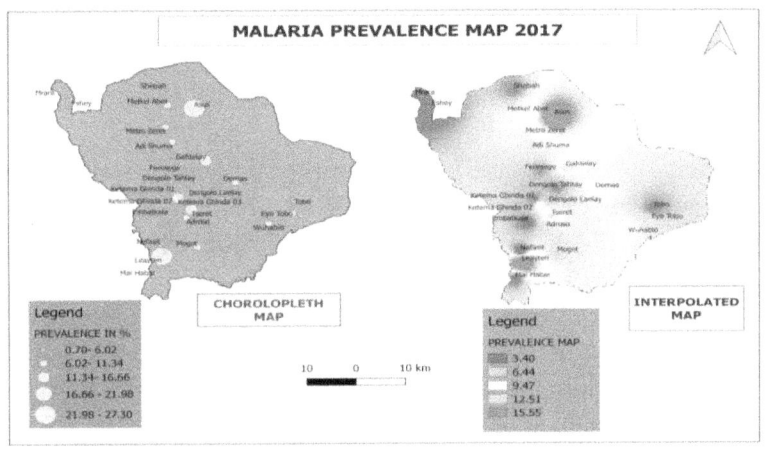

Figure 11. Malaria prevalence map and its interpolated form, 2017.

6. Discussion

Although successful eradication of malaria has been achieved in many Ne'us Zobas in Eritrea, where it was alarming not so long ago (last 15 years), the situation is still problematic in Ne'us Zoba Ghindae. Malaria remains both highly endemic and epidemic in significant areas of Ne'us Zoba Ghindae, possibly due to its natural climate, landscape and environmental conditions in favor of mosquito breeding and malaria transmission. Moreover, a recent resurgence of malaria has been noted in some parts of the Ne'us Zoba attributed to diverse aspects, which include entomological, epidemiological, bio-physical, topographical, and socio-economic factors.

The Ne'us Zoba is characterized by wide elevation range (118 to 2048 mts. above seas level), moderate to high mean annual temperature (17.9°C to 28.3°C) and bimodal rainfall pattern. Due to the wide range of eco-epidemiological settings, malaria in Ne'us Zoba Ghindae can be coarsely grouped into three epidemiologic zones, considering altitude, and settlements' rural-urban setting. However, within settlements, there may be variations in malaria epidemiology and thus the epidemiologic zonation at times may overlap. The epidemiologic zones are discussed below.

i.   Rural Lowland malaria: It is common in settlements located mostly in the lowland part of the Ne'us Zoba (below 1500mts. above sea level) and floodplain areas and is mainly attributable to water-resources development areas (e.g., irrigation). Moreover, pockets of sustained malaria transmission persist particularly near moderate and small-scale irrigation schemes, probably associated with low water management skill of the local people.

ii.   Urban (and Semi-urban) malaria: Ne'us Zoba Ghindae is primarily rural, with few small towns and semi-towns dotted along the main Asmara-Massawa highway that runs through the center of Ne'us Zoba Ghindae, including the town of Ghindae. Interestingly, Ghindae town has an area of about 4.44 sq.km, with high population density of about 6,000 persons/ sq. km. This high density, especially in some slum-like neighborhoods of Ghindae town, may accelerate malaria infections. Moreover, significant portion of the town is transversed by Mai-Adkemom stream, flowing almost the whole year, probably leading to intensified malaria. In the epidemic year of 2016, about half (49%) of the passive malaria infection was in Ghindae town. Thus, malaria can no longer be considered as just a rural issue in the Ne'us Zoba under consideration, although the malaria risk nationwide in Eritrea is comparatively lower in urban areas than in rural areas (Berhane *et al.*, 2015).

iii. Rural Highland Malaria: This is malaria eco-epidemiologic region, mainly in localities found in above 1500 mts. above sea level, which is historically malaria-free. However, recently the incidence of highland malaria, in some parts of the study area, is noticeable. The highland villages of the Ne'us Zoba are populated by more than 10,000 people, with low immunity to malaria and, hence at high risk. More recently (September to October, 2017), there was an elevated incidence of malaria in highland fringe village ofLayten of Ne'us Zoba Ghindae, probably due to the population movement from the malarious areas carrying the vector with them, or local micro-geographic situations suiting malaria transmission.

7. Conclusion

In Eritrea, the country being in the pre-elimination stage and with changing epidemiological pattern of malaria, where malaria is at low transmission intensity, the need to explore alternative approaches of malaria risk estimation becomes important. Thus, in this study, by using weighted multi-criteria analysis, guided by outputs from sensitivity analysis of individual factor influence and taking into consideration weighting of factors by previous researchers, a GIS raster-based model was generated producing malaria risk map of Ne'us Zoba Ghindae. The developed mapping database and techniques in this research work are expected to greatly assist the health department of the study area in fighting malaria. More importantly, the potentiality of geospatial data, such as remotely sensed data cannot be ignored, as it is cost effective, accurate and less time consuming for manipulating malaria risk mapping.

References

Ahmad, F., Goparaju, L., & Qayum, A. (2017). Studying malaria epidemic for vulnerability zones: Multi-criteria approach of geospatial tools. *Journal of Geoscience and Environment Protection, 5* (5), 30-53.

Balls M. J., Bodker, R., Thomas, C. J., Kisinza, W., Msangeni, H. A., & Lindsay, S. W. (2004). Effect of topography on the risk of malaria infection in the Usambara Mountains, Tanzania. *Transactions of the Royal Society of Tropical Medicine and Hygiene, 98*(7), 400-408.

Berhane, A., Mihreteab, S., Ahmed, H., Zehaie, A., Abdulmumini U., & Chanda E. (2015). Gains attained in malaria control coverage within settings embarked for pre-elimination: malaria indicator and prevalence surveys 2012, Eritrea, *Malaria Journal, 14*, 467-477.

Berhane, A., Russom M., Bahta, I., Hagos, F., Ghirmai M., & Uqubay, S. (2017). Rapid diagnostic tests failing to detect *Plasmodium falciparum* infections in Eritrea: An investigation of reported false negative RDT results, *Malaria Journal, 16*, 105-118.

Bi, P., Tong, S., Donald, K., Parton, K., & Ni, J. (2003). Climatic variables and transmission of malaria: A 12 years data analysis in Schuchen County, China. *Public Health Reports, 118*(1), 65-71.

Ceccato, P., Ghebremeskel, T., Jaitech, M., Graves, P. M., Levy, M., Ghebreselassie, S., Ogbamariam, A., Barnston, A.

G., Bell, M., del Corral, J., Connor, S. J., Fesseha, I., Brantly, E. P., Thomson, M. C. (2007). Malaria stratification, climate and epidemic early warning in Eritrea. *American Journal of Tropical Medicine and Hygiene, 77*(6), 61-68.

Chanda, E., Mihreteab, S., Berhane, A., Zehaie, A., Yohannes, G., & Abdulmumini, U. (2015). Consolidating strategic planning and operational frameworks for integrated vector management in Eritrea. *Malaria Journal, 14*, 488-501.

Chikodzi, D. (2013). Spatial modelling of malaria risk zones using environmental, anthropogenic variables and GIS techniques. *Journal of Geosciences and Geomatics, 1*(1), 8-14.

Craig M. H., Snow, R. W., & Le Sueur, D. (1999). A climate-based distribution model of malaria transmission in Africa. *Parasitology Today, 15*(3), 105-111.

De Silva, P. M., & Marshall, J. M. (2012). Factors contributing to urban malaria transmission in Sub-Saharan Africa: A systematic review. *Journal of Tropical Medicine,* 819563, 1-10.

Graves, P. M. (2004). Eritrea: Malaria surveillance, epidemic preparedness, and control program strengthening. Environmental Health Project, Activity Report 144. http://www.ehproject.org/PDF/Activity_Reports/AR%201 44%20Eritrea%20Activity%20Report%20FORMAT.pdf.

Habtai, H., Ghebremeskel, T., Mihreteab S., Mufunda, J., & Gebremichael, A. (2009). Knowledge, attitudes and practices (KAP) about malaria among people visiting referral hospitals of Eritrea in 2008. *Journal of Eritrean Medical Association, 4*(1), 42-46.

Hanafi-Bojd, A. A., Vatandoost, H., Oshaghi, M. A., Charrahy, Z., Haghdoost, A. A., Zamani, G., Abedi, F., Sedaghat, M. M., Soltani, M., Shahi, M., Raeisi, A. (2012). Spatial analysis and mapping of malaria risk in an endemic area, south of Iran: A GIS based decision making for planning of control. *Acta Tropica, 122*(1), 132-137.

Kaya, S., Pultz, T. J., Mbogo, C. M., Beier, J. C., & Mushinzimana, E. (2001). The use of Radar remote sensing for identifying environmental factors associated with malaria risk in coastal Kenya. Submitted to the International Geoscience and Remote Sensing Symposium (IGARSS '02), Toronto, June 24-28, 2002.

Keating, J., Localetti, A., Ghebremicheal, A., Ghebremekel, T., Mufunda, J., Mihreteab, S., Berhane, D., & Carneiro, P. (2011). Evaluating indoor residual spray for reducing malaria infection prevalence in Eritrea: Results from a community randomized control trial. *Acta Tropica, 119*(2 & 3), 107-113.

Meron, M. (2010). Web GIS in decision support to control malaria: Case study in Tiro-Afeta Woreda, Oromia, Ethiopia. M.Sc. Thesis, Addis Ababa University, Addis Ababa.

Meron, M., Tsega, T., Teklemariam, A., Mengesteab, T. (2018). Malaria risk stratification and modelling, the effect of rainfall on malaria incidence in Eritrea, Unpublished article.

Ministry of Health (2016), State of Eritrea. State of Eritrea Health Management Information System (HMIS), Unpublished Report.

Ministry of Health (2016), State of Eritrea. State of Eritrea, Annual Health Sector Report.

Mohammed, A. O., Tewelde, S., Estifanos, D., Tekeste, Y., Osman, M.-H. (2018). Therapeutic efficacy of artesunate-amiodaquine for treating uncomplicated falciparum malaria at Ghindae Zonal Referral Hospital, Eritrea. *Acta Tropica, 177*, 94-96.

Mushinzimana, E., Munga, S., Minakawa, N., Li, L., Feng, C.-C., Bian, L., Kitron, U., Schmidt, C., Beck, L., Zhou, G., Githeko, A. K., & Yan, G. (2006) Landscape determinants and remote sensing of mosquito larval habitats in the highlands of Kenya. *Malaria Journal, 5,* 13-24.

Negasi, F. (2008). Identifying, mapping and evaluating environmental factors affecting malaria transmission using GIS and RS in selected Kebeles of Adama district, Oromia Region. M.Sc. Thesis, Addis Ababa University, Addis Ababa.

Nyarango, P. M., Gebremeskel, T., Mebrahtu, G., Mufanda, J., Abdulmumini, U., Ogbamariam, A., Kosia, A., Gebremichael, A., Gunawardena, D., Ghebrat, Y., & Okbaldet Y. (2006). A steep decline in malaria morbidity and mortality trends in Eritrea between 2000 and 2004: the effect of a combination of control methods. *Malaria Journal*, *5*(1), 33-46.

Shililu, J., Ghebremeskel, T., Mengistu, S., Fekadu, H., Zerom, M., Mbogo, C., Githure, J., Gu, W., Novak, R., & Beier, J. C. (2003). Distribution of anopheline mosquitoes in Eritrea. *American Journal of Tropical Medicine and Hygiene*, *69*(3), 295-302.

Shililu, J., Ghebremeskel, T., Seulu, F., Mengistu, S., Fekadu, H., Zerom, M., Asmelash, G. E., Sintasath, D., Mbogo, C., Githure, J., Brantly, E., Beier, J.C., & Novak, R. J. (2004). Seasonal abundance, vector behavior, and malaria parasite transmission in Eritrea. *Journal of American Mosquito Control Association*, *20*(2), 155-164.

Shook, G. (1997). An assessment of disaster risk and its management in Thailand. *Disasters*, *21*(1), 77-88.

Sintasath, M., Ghebremeskel, T., Lynch, M., Kleinau, E., Bretas, G., Shililu, J., Brantly, E., Graves, P. M., & Beier, J.C. (2005). Malaria prevalence and associated risk factors in Eritrea. *American Journal of Tropical Medicine and Hygiene*, *72*(6), 682-687.

Stratton, L., O'Neille, M. S., Kruk, M. E., & Bell, M. L. (2008). The persistent problem of malaria: Addressing the fundamental causes of a global killer. *Social Science & Medicine*, *67*(5), 857-862.

Tanser, de F. C., Sharp, B., & Sueur, D. le, (2003). Potential effect of climate change on malaria transmission in Africa. *Lancet*, *362*, 1792-1798.

World Health Organization [WHO] (2017). World Malaria Report, Geneva.

World Health Organization, [WHO] (2003). World Malaria Report, Geneva.

Yukich J. O., Zerom, M., Ghebremeskel, T., Tediosi, F., & Lengeler, C. (2009). Costs and cost-effectiveness of vector control in Eritrea using insecticide-treated bed nets. *Malaria Journal*, *8*(1), 1-14.

Zewga, M. (2016). Malaria risk assessment using GIS and remote sensing: A case study of Kewet Wereda, North Shewa Zone, Amhara Region. M.Sc. Thesis, Addis Ababa University, Addis Ababa.

Assessment of Land Degradation Vulnerability through Land Use/Land Cover Change Detection in Tsmieti Catchment, Ne'us Zoba Adi Kuala

Mebrahtom Zerom[1] and Ogbaghebriel Berakhi[†]

Abstract

Land degradation is a major environmental problem in Eritrea, particularly within the highland regions, where Tsmieti catchment is found. The heavy dependence of peoples' lives on agriculture and other land-related activities coupled with inappropriate use of environmental resources resulted in rapid and widespread land degradation. The growing population pressure has caused land cover change by clearing trees and shrubs for the expansion of agriculture into the fragile, unsuitable areas. This study is aimed at assessing the current situation of land degradation in Tsmieti catchment, found in Ne'us Zoba Adi Kuala, Eritrea based on land use/land cover (LULC) change analysis. Landsat images taken at three points in time (1994, 2002, and 2015) were classified into five LULC classes using supervised classification technique by utilizing QGIS2.18. Then, post classification change detection and Normalized Difference Vegetation Index (NDVI) were computed for examining the spatio-temporal changes in the land scenario.The results of LULC change detection show that, classes of rain-fed and irrigated croplands, degraded lands and built-up area are expanding in areal coverage at the expense of grazing land, which include open tree cover area, shrub land and grasslands. Accordingly, the quantitatively computed values reveal that rain-fed cropland, irrigated lands, degraded lands and built-up area show positive percentage changes of 49%, 64.8%, 100.2% and 106.6% respectively, while grazing land is declined by 59%. The areal share of degraded land

[1] Lecturer, Department of Geography, College of Business and Social Sciences, Eritrea. E-mail: mebzerom20@yahoo.com/esseymebrahtom@gmail.com.

[†] Dr. Ogbaghebriel Berakhi was for many years a senior lecturer at the Department of Georgrahy until his passing in 2021 and, between 2010 and 2015, he was the dean of the College of Arts and Social Sciences in Adi QeyyiH. He also served in other senior academic capacities earlier.

was 296 ha in 1994, 381ha in 2002 and 593ha in 2015. Currently, degraded lands account for 8.8% of the study area, while NDVI image comparisons also indicate major decline in land cover of the study area in the meantime. Thus, the finding of the study calls proper conservation intervention and the information is also relevant to the national and international sustainable development goals.

Keywords: Land degradation; LULC change; NDVI; Tsmieti catchment; Ne'us Zoba Adi Kuala; Eritrea.

1. Introduction

Land degradation remains an important global agenda in the 21st century because of its adverse impact on agronomic productivity, the environment, and its effect on food security and the quality of life (Eswaran *et al.*, 2001). Despite the emerging recognition of the importance of environmental resources for the survival of humanity on the planet, the environment is being degraded at an alarming rate (Yimer, 2015). Consequently, the world is getting seriously confronted by issues of sustainable use of environmental resources. The problem is more acute and diverse in Africa. An estimated 65% of Africa's agricultural land is degraded and threatens millions of people with starvation. In addition, 31% of the continent's pasture lands and 19% of its forests and woodlands are classified as degraded (FAO, 2005; ELD & UNEP, 2015).

In Eritrea, natural resources such as land, water, and forest are essential to the survival and livelihood of the population. However, land degradation has become a serious problem affecting all spheres of social, economic and political life of the population. Currently, land degradation is one of the most pressing challenges to agricultural development and food security in the country. Different studies suggest that a large proportion of Eritrea's land is degraded (Woldetinsae *et al.*, 2005; Bai *et al.*, 2008; AMESD, 2011). According to these studies, 35-39% of the land of Eritrea, mainly the highlands is degraded. This highly degraded central highland covers 16% of the land of the country, but accommodates about 65% of the total population and 23% of the total livestock in Eritrea (MoA, 2002).

The major drivers of land degradation in Eritrean highlands are human activities, including deforestation, mismanagement of arable land, cultivation on steep slopes, overgrazing and lack of proper conservation measures. Natural factors like topography and concurrent drought are also among the commonly cited reasons. However, the principal factor for the degradation of land is land use/land cover (LULC) change caused by population pressure. According to a 2002 report of MoA, the overall average population density of the country was 9.2 persons/ha or 0.11 ha/capita of cropland in that time. This value would become less favorable as population increases in the subsequent years but size of the land remains constant.

LULC change, which is an issue of global environmental change (Gashaw *et al.*, 2014) is also major environmental problem in Eritrea. Land cover (LC) is the observed biophysical cover or type of features present on the land surface, like vegetation cover and man-made structures. Whereas, the term land use (LU), generally refers to the human use and modification of the land or economic function associated with a specific piece of land. Small-scale agriculture, grazing, industrial zone and residential use, are examples of some land use types (Campbell & Wynne, 2011; Lillesand *et al.*, 2015; Yengoh *et al.*, 2015; Stellmes *et al.*, 2015). Land use change is the alteration in the use of a particular land from one type to another over time, e.g., from shrub lands to arable land, arable land to grazing, etc. (Gashaw *et al.*, 2014; Stellmes *et al.*, 2015). The assessment of LULC conversion is often based on land use change detection performed at defined years of interest. The identification is carried out by comparing two maps representing the same region, but depict land use patterns at different dates, which are compared point by point to summarize the difference between the two dates (Campbell & Wynne, 2011).

The study area, Tsmieti catchment, situated within Ne'us Zoba Adi Kuala, is part of the highland region of the country where topography is mountainous and undulating, with poor vegetation cover. Traditional agricultural practices are a means of sustenance for almost the entire population of the Ne'us Zoba. However, as mentioned above, the combined effect of such processes lead in decline of land capability, and land degradation is threatening the area thereby affecting livelihood of the population negatively. The urge to produce enough food for the increasing population, has resulted in clearing of trees and shrubs for the expansion of agriculture into the fragile, unsuitable areas and this has been leading to serious deforestation and soil erosion conditions.

Though it is difficult to assess fully the dimensions of land degradation (deforestation; the focus of this study) in terms of extent and magnitude, Remote Sensing (RS) and Geographic Information System (GIS) techniques provide a suitable and systematic approach for obtaining the spatial and temporal information so important in the assessment of land degradation. Despite their benefits, the application of such technologies in assessment and monitoring of land degradation have not been fully utilized in Eritrea.

Thus, land use/land cover change detection using remotely sensed satellite images are very crucial in identifying vulnerability to land degradation, so that integrated mitigation measures could be undertaken. The main objective of the study is to identify land degradation in the form of deforestation by looking into LULC changes over time and space. Specific objectives include; (i) to map the current LULC patterns of the study area and to model their spatio-temporal changes, (ii) to quantify the spatial extent of degraded lands in the area.

2. Materials and methods

A. Study area

The study area, Tsmieti catchment, is located within Ne'us Zoba Adi Kuala, between 14° 33' 08" N to 14° 36' 58" N latitude and 38° 43' 02" E to 38° 52' 57" E longitude (Figure 1). It has a total area of 67.4 sq. km (6735ha) which accounts for 9% of the total area of the Ne'us Zoba. The elevation of the area ranges from 1444 to 2138 mts.. Mean annual rainfall of the area is 623mm and the annual min-max temperature records are 8°C and 33°C. The catchment is drained by Tsmieti River which originates at about 7kms to east of the Adi Kuala, the major town and administrative center of the Ne'us Zoba.

The Ne'us Zoba has the largest population of 98,703 in Zoba Debub and 96.2% of the population relies on traditional subsistence farming (MoA, Ne'us Zoba Adi Kuala, 2016; Zoba Debub Statistics office, 2016). The overall population density of Ne'us Zoba Adi Kuala is 132 persons/km^2, but the agricultural population density (the farming population divided by the available cultivable land) is 456 persons/km^2. The study area is characterized by different LULC types, mainly farm lands, irrigated lands, scattered trees, shrubs and grasslands and some artificial structures as well as bare lands. Farm lands are dominating mainly the flat and gentle slopes of the area and irrigated lands are limited along the major waterways. Areas which are not suitable for crop cultivation are devoted for grazing purposes.

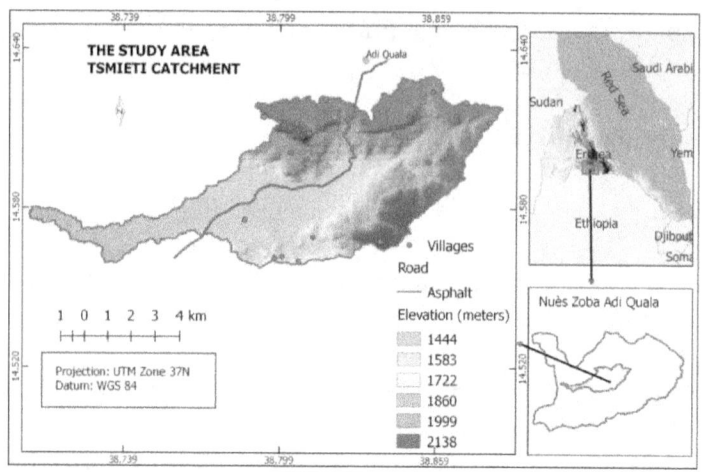

Figure 11. Location of the study area.

B. Data collection

Both primary and secondary data sets were utilized. The primary data include, data generated from remote sensing techniques and collected from the field. Landsat images are among the widely used satellite remote sensing data for LULC research. Hence, Landsat data taken at three points in time (see for details in the table below) that cover the study area were used for mapping and modeling the spatio-temporal changes of LULC patterns. Besides, for easing the interpretation of the Landsat images, a high resolution QuickBird Images, with 0.6m resolution, acquired on Nov. 2009, was obtained from Eritrean Mapping and Information Center (EMIC). Moreover, GoogleEarth images were used for assisting the interpretation of the historic images. A 30m resolution Digital Elevation Model (DEM) was also obtained from EMIC. Field reference data, used for image classification and accuracy assessment were collected using GPS receivers. On the other hand, secondary data like climatic data, vector data sets and information on population were collected from different offices, books, journals and reports.

Data	Acqui sition Date	Sensor	Path/ Row	Spat ial Res.	Image ID	Clou d %
Main Data	Nov. 2, 1994	TM5	169/50	30m	LT51690501994306xxx02	*2.35
	Nov. 16, 2002	ETM+7	169/50	30m	LE71690502002320SGS00	0
	Nov. 28, 2015	OLI_TIR8	169/50	30m	LC81690502015332LGN00	0

Table 12. Characteristics of the Landsat data.
* Cloud % presence for the study area is 0%.

i. Sampling technique for collection of field reference data

An approach of stratified purposive sampling was chosen for collecting field reference data. Reference data were taken for each LULC category in the field by moving in a traverse way in north-south and/or east-west directions. The researchers took a reference point of a class at a specific starting site, and then, at every certain distance (roughly 100 mts.) intervals as he walked in a given direction. In this manner, a total of 620 reference data were collected for the predefined LULC classes. Finally, 70% of the total collected points were used for training purpose in the classification and the rest 30% were used for validation of the classification result. Selection of the points used for accuracy purpose was based on systematic sampling.

C. Methods

i. Pre-processing and classification scheme for LULC mapping

Digital image processing involves the manipulation and interpretation of digital images with the help of a computer (Lillesand *et al.*, 2015). Image pre-processing technique is aimed to correct distorted or degraded image data to create a more faithful representation of the original scene. It improves an image's utility for further manipulation. Effective image pre-processing is therefore, critical to successful LULC mapping and change detection (Tewolde & Cabral, 2011). Though some basic processing has already been done by the United States Geological Survey (USGS), additional image pre-processing of all the satellite images used for this study was done in the GRASS software 7.2.0 and then taken to QGIS 2.18 for further analysis.

Image classification is performed with a set of target classes in mind; these sets are called classification scheme or system (Tewolde & and Cabral, 2011). Hence, by having applied the techniques of image classification, LULC types were identified, and the change detection was computed. The classification scheme was adopted from GLOBCOVER (2009) classification system, but modifications were made to fit to local conditions. The details of the major LULC classes are presented as follows.

LULC class	Simplified description based on GLOBCOVER classes
rain-fed cropland	area cultivated during rainy months of the year when the dry season is on fallow
irrigated cropland	permanently cultivated lands with fruit plantations and vegetable fields
grazing land	This includes all areas covered with grasses, shrub and sparse tree cover. This land is predominantly used for grazing
degraded/barren land	all lands covered mainly by bare soil and exposed rock surfaces
built-up or artificial surface	This includes the visible human infrastructure, like buildings, roads and accumulated hay.

Table 13. *LULC classes scheme for the study area.*

ii. Image classification and accuracy assessment

Visual image interpretation, which gives a general understanding about the area under investigation, was done by observing the different color composites. Analysis of LULC was done at composite band of the visible (true color) and near infrared bands (false color). Each band is sensitive to a different part of the reflected solar energy and many earth features manifest very distinctive spectral reflectance in these bands (Figure 2). Hence, image classification is done to replace visual interpretation of image data with quantitative techniques for automating the identification of features in a scene (Lillesand *et al.*, 2015). It is the process of assigning all pixels in an image into LULC classes or themes (Campbell & Wynne, 2011; Tewolde & Cabral, 2011). Pixels that share similar combinations of spectral reflectance or emissivity are grouped together in classes that represent a particular surface feature.

Image classification is a complex and time consuming process, and the result of the classification is likely to be affected by a variety of factors like availability of reference data, complexity of landscape, and algorithms used (Araya & Hergarten, 2008). To overcome this complexity, various classification methods have been developed, such as pixel based, sub-pixel, and object based approaches. Thus, selection of appropriate classification method is required, for successful analysis of change detection. Pixel based supervised image classification approach with maximum likelihood classifier algorithm, that relies on spectral differences of surface features has been utilized. Training sites were established based on the field reference points collected during field work. The training area describes the spectral attributes of each feature type. Each pixel in the data set (image) is then compared numerically to each category in the reference data (training areas) and assigned to a category looks most alike.

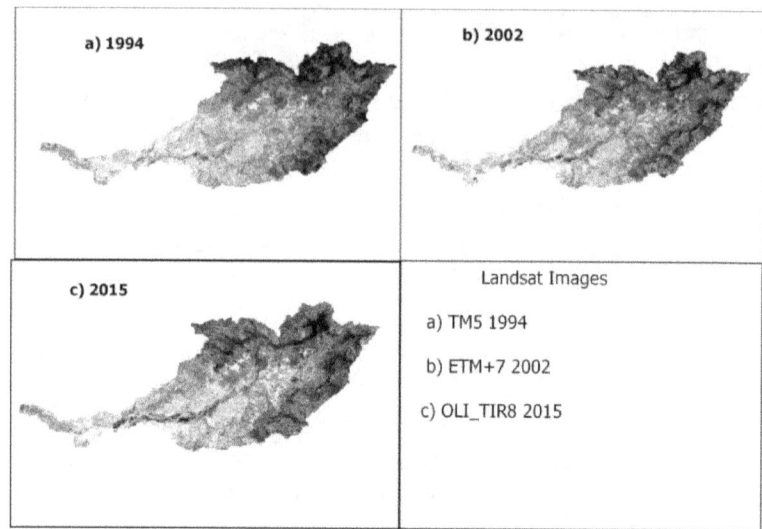

Figure 12. False color image contrasts of the study periods, where vegetation appears in reddish color.

Accuracy assessment is a process used to check the accuracy of classification result by comparing the classified map with a reference map (Araya & Cabral, 2010). This step is very important in justifying the accuracy and reliability of the classification results and currently, it is considered as an integral part of any image classification process.

The most common and standard way of representing classification accuracy is in the form of an error matrix, sometimes also called a confusion matrix. An error matrix is a square array of rows and columns and presents the relationship between known reference data (verification data) and the corresponding results of the classification. Accuracy assessment in this study was computed, by comparing the resultant classified map and a set of field reference data (182 points), using Semi-Automatic Classification tool (SCP) in QGIS. The value of each class in the classified image were compared and verified against the reference data. The overall accuracy, including user's and producer's accuracy were calculated from the matrix. Moreover, the Kappa coefficient, one of the most popular measures of addressing the difference between actual agreement and chance agreement was computed using the equation below and the information contained in Table 3.

$$K = \frac{N \sum_{i=1}^{r} xii - \sum_{i=1}^{r}(xi_+ * x+1)}{N^2 - \sum_{i=1}^{r}(xi_+ * x+1)}$$

(Kappa Coefficient adopted from Lillesand *et al.*, 2015)

where:

r = number of rows in the matrix

Xii = number of observations in rows i and column i (along the major diagonal)

Xi_+ = the marginal total of row i (shown at the right of the matrix)

$X+1$ = the marginal total of column i (shown at the bottom of the matrix)

N = total number of observations in the matrix

The overall methodological steps employed are summarized below in the form of flow chart (Figure3).

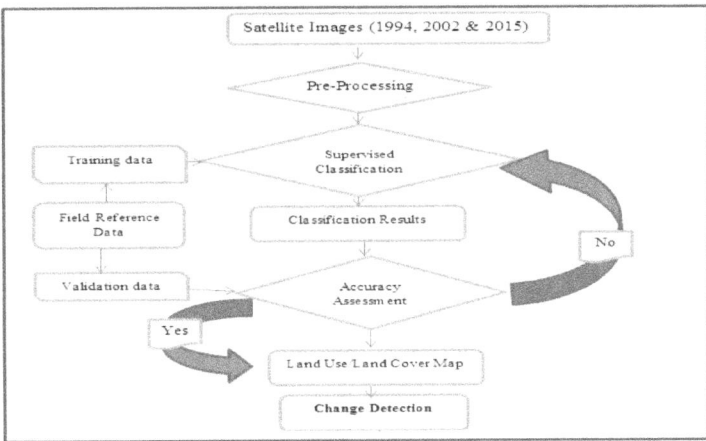

Figure 13. Methodological flow chart.

iii. Post classification change detection

Change detection is among the most powerful advantages of remote sensing images. According to Lillesand *et al.* (2015), change detection involves the use of multi-temporal data sets to discriminate areas of land cover change between dates of imaging. One way of discriminating change over time is to employ post classification comparison. This kind of change detection method identifies and provides where and how much change has occurred. In this approach, two dates of imagery are independently classified and registered. Then an algorithm is employed to determine those pixels whose class changed between the dates. Similarly, the evaluation of the change detection made in this study was based on the standard requirements; the three satellite images taken in 1994, 2002 and 2015 were classified into identical LULC classes. Then after, change detection between the classified images was done using SCP tool. The change matrix (cross matrix) of LULC change between 1994 and 2015 was also computed to see the detailed transformation of class value (cell value) from one class type to another class.

In addition, the Normalized Difference Vegetation Index (NDVI), one of the most common vegetation indices used for assessing vegetation cover of an area over different time periods, was also computed. Studies have proven that NDVI can be used as a proxy for assessing changes in vegetation cover in an area. It can help in identifying deforestation, its rate and the area affected (Yengoh *et al.*, 2015). NDVI empirical formula is based on the difference of reflectance in the near-infrared and red bands of the electromagnetic spectrum. This spectral vegetation index permits clear discrimination between vegetated and non-vegetated surfaces. High NDVI values will be obtained from an area of green vegetation, where there is high reflectance in the near infrared and low reflectance in the red band. Hence, NDVI values of 1994 and 2015 images were calculated as follows using QGIS raster calculator.

$$NDVI = (NIR - RED)/(NIR + RED)$$

where NIR is the near infrared band response for a given pixel and RED is the red band response of the same pixel.

3. Results and discussion

A. Classification results and accuracy assessment

The LULC maps, derived through pixel based supervised classification technique are depicted below (Figure 4). The validation of these maps, which is an essential step to carry out further change analysis, was calculated as shown in (Table 3). The overall accuracy of the classified map of 2015 is 85.16%. In some empirical studies, it is noted that a minimum accuracy value of 85% is required for effective and reliable land cover change analysis and modeling. Hence, the classification carried out in this study produces an overall accuracy level that fulfills the minimum accuracy threshold defined by Anderson *et al.* (1976). Besides, due to the unavailability of reference data for the years 1994 and 2002 images, the same level of accuracy was assumed, since the same procedures and algorithms were applied.

The producer's accuracy, which is also referred as error of omission, measures the probability of a reference pixel being classified correctly. It ranges from 63% to 100% (see Table 3). Built-up area shows the lowest producer's accuracy, as many pixels belonging to it are mistakenly classified into the other class types. This is mainly attributed to the similarity in spectral properties with some other land cover classes, especially with bare lands and grazing land (open tree cover), as many villages are having planted trees (like eucalyptus). User's accuracy which evaluates the probability that the pixels in classified image

117

represent that class on the ground ranges from 80% to 92% (Table 3). The degraded barren land has lowest user's accuracy of 80%, which means that only 80% of this class is correctly identified and to some extent it is misclassified, as rain-fed cropland (gain more points). This is probably caused by the similarity in the spectral signature of the features.

Moreover, the Kappa value for classified image 2015 was 0.803, which is considered to be good and reliable for LULC change analysis. The Kappa value is segmented into three categories. A value greater than 0.8 represent strong agreement, 0.4 - 0.8 indicates moderate agreement and that of less than 0.4 is considered as poor agreement. The Kappa value expresses the proportionate reduction in error generated by a classification process compared with the error of a completely random classification (Lillesand et al., 2015).

Row labels	Rain-fed cropland	Irrigated Cropland	Grazing land	Bare land	Built-up	Row Total	User's Accuracy (%)
rain-fed cropland	49	0	4	3	2	58	84.482758
irrigated cropland	0	11	1	0	0	12	91.666667
grazing land	2	0	51	0	8	61	83.606557
bare land	1	0	1	21	3	26	80.769231
built-up	1	0	0	1	23	25	92
column total	53	11	57	25	36	182	
Producer's accuracy (%)	92.45283	100	89.473684	84	63.888889		Overall Accuracy 85.16

Table 14. Error matrix of the classified image 2015.

During the classification processes, irrigated and bare land classes were comparatively easily identifiable with the help of some ancillary data. On the other hand, some tree-covered areas in the image were treated as irrigated lands due to similarity in their spectral signature. Similarly, the distinction between rain-fed cropland and areas of grass lands were not simple and took several iterations. Above all, the most difficult task was in discriminating the built-up area, particularly where the nature of the settlement is dispersed and when villages have eucalyptus plants.

The visual interpretation of the satellite images given abovein false color composite (Figure 2), show great disparities in the land cover characteristics of the area prior to the classification process. The satellite image of 1994 (Figure 2a) shows the presence of good land cover, since vegetation appears as bright red in false color composite. The proportion of the land cover (red color) decreases greatly in the subsequent images (Figure 2b, c). Similarly, the result of the classification demonstrates this fact, where significant changes are observed in the classified images of the meantime. To substantiate this, the extent of each LULC class in the study years was computed and quantified (see Table 4). Land cover; the grazing land which incorporates open tree cover, shrubs and grass covered area took the highest proportion in the 1994 classified image, but it was reduced by half in the later classified image of 2015 (Figure 5). It is important to mention that the study put the different land cover types (open tree cover, shrub land, bush land and grass lands) in to one class of grazing lands, understanding the level of difficulty in discriminating such features in the field during the process of reference data collection and to avoid intrusion of subjective bias in final results.

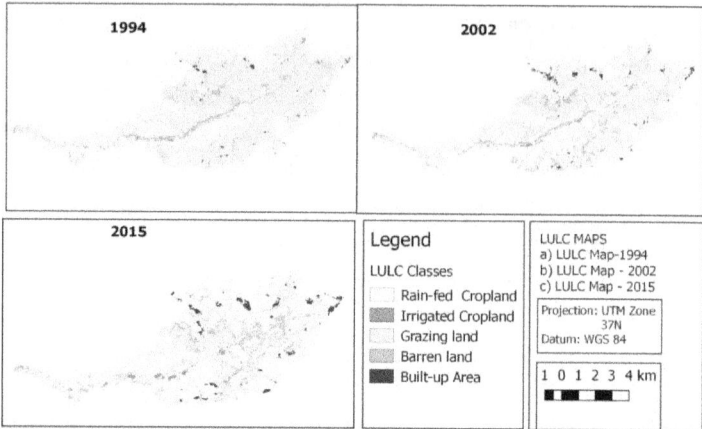

Figure 14. Land Use/Land Cover maps of 1994, 2002 and 2015.

The areal proportion of each LULC classes of the study area under the study years is depicted graphically in Figure 5.

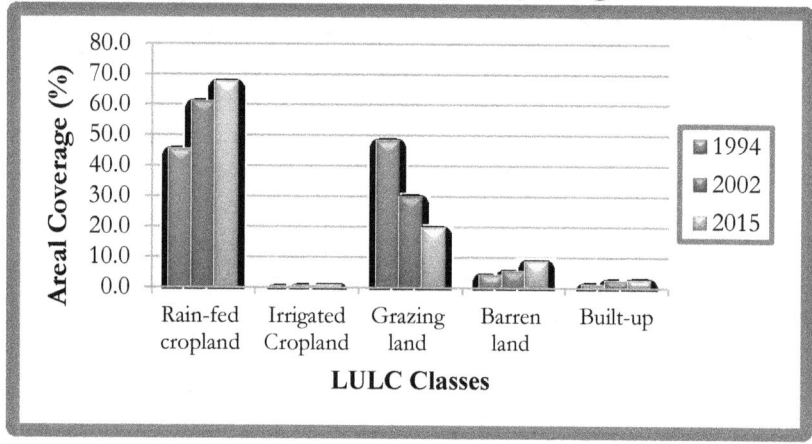

Figure 15. Patterns of Land use/land cover change.

B. Post classification smoothing

Classified data often produces a salt and pepper appearance (small isolated pixels) due to the inherent spectral variability encountered by the classifier when applied on a pixel-by-pixel basis (Lillesand *et al.*, 2015). Thus, smoothing often is applied to show only the dominant and correct classifications. One method of classification smoothing involves the application of a majority filter. In this method a moving window is passed through the classified data set and the majority class within the window is determined. This method was adopted in this study to remove the isolated pixels from the dominant class type. Hence, Classification Sieve was applied, where the Minimum Mapping Unit (MMU) corresponds to three pixels (area of 8100 mt^2). Pixel value with an area smaller than the defined MMU would be replaced by the largest neighboring class. MMU refers to the smallest size area to be mapped as a discrete area (Lillesand *et al.*, 2015). As such, all class area smaller than defined MMU in the classified images, were replaced by the dominant nearby class type.

C. Post classification change analysis and quantification

The terms land use and land cover are sometimes used interchangeably, but they refer to fundamentally different concepts. Land cover is the biophysical features present on the surface of the earth. The term land use however, refers to human use and modification of specific piece of land. Change in LULC in general and land cover in particular would have either direct or indirect impacts on the extent and conditions of land degradation. Such changes could be transformation of land cover to land use, from one land use to another land use or from land use to land cover. In this way, LULC change can serve as pointers to the existence or absence of land degradation. Despite this fact, it is difficult to conclude that whenever there is change in LULC, such change could be eventually followed by land degradation. However, as Maitima *et al.*, (2009) argues, if LULC change is towards cultivated and degraded lands, the soil is easily susceptible to erosion than soils in forest, shrubs and grasslands do and finally it may lead to land degradation.

Similarly, the increasing population pressure in the study area, in line with some socio-economic and political conditions of the country, resulted in LULC change, which in turn has led to change in environmental systems. Results of the quantification of areal extent of individual classes and the magnitude of change presented in hectares and percentage (Table 4) indicate a considerable amount of change, where classes of rain-fed and degraded lands expanded tremendously while grazing lands shrunk a lot. The magnitude of change for each LULC class was determined as follows and the results are given in (Table 4) below.

$$\text{Rate of change (ha/yr.)} = (X-Y)/Z$$

whereXis the recent area of a LULC in ha. and Y is the previous area of a LULC in ha., while Z is the time interval between X and Y in years.

Beside this, the percentage change of LULC classes among the classified satellite images under study time was also calculated as

$$\text{Percentage change} = (X-Y)/Y * 100$$

where X is the recent area of a LULC (ha) and Y is the previous area of a LULC (ha).

According to the results given in Table 4, rain-fed cropland witnessed a great positive change, with almost 50 percent increment between 1994 and 2015. Initially, this class accounts for 45% of the areal in 1994. This figure rose to 61% and 68% in 2002 and 2015, respectively. This is perhaps associated with an increase in population of the area that further led an increase in the demand of agricultural lands. This is further supported by the highest positive change in the built-up area that has gained more than one hundred percent increment rate from 1994 to 2015

(Figure 6). Irrigated cropland has also recorded a positive change, with 65% enlargement from 1994 to 2015. In the initial classified image of 1994, the proportion of this class was 38 ha (0.6%) but later increased to 63 ha (1%) in the LULC map of 2015 (Table 4).

	1994		2002		2015		1994-2002		2002-2015		199
	Area (ha)	Area %	Area (ha)	Area %	Area (ha)	Area %	Rate of change	% change	Rate of change	% change	Rate of change
	3056	45.38	4117	61.13	4562	67.72	133	35	34	11	72
	38	0.57	43	0.64	63	0.94	1	13	1.5	46	1
d	3255	48.33	2019	29.98	1334	19.81	-155	-38	-53	-34	-91
ad	296	4.40	381	5.66	593	8.81	11	28	16	56	14
	89	1.32	175	2.59	183	2.72	11	97	1	5	5
	6735	100	6735	100	6735	100					

Table 15. Area of LULC classes in 1994, 2002 and 2015 and their magnitude of change.

Grazing land which incorporates area of open tree cover, thicket, shrub land and grass lands is the only LULC class which shows a very high net loss (Figure 6). In 1994, this class took the highest proportion, 48%. However, the class was continually pushed particularly by agricultural practices and degradation with a rate loss of 91 ha per year. Its areal share in the latest classified image of 2015 is reduced to 20% only. In other words, 91 ha of land coved by trees, shrubs and/or grasses were deforested and/or converted to other land use classes every year. The class shows negative 59% reduction rate from 1994 to 2015. In the 21 year of study period, a total of 1921 ha of land cover were estimated to be converted to other land use types (Figure 6). As discussed earlier, the conversion of land cover towards cultivation and bare land will ultimately make the land more vulnerable to land degradation.

The main reasons for massive conversion of grazing land include the ever increasing demand of farm lands and cutting of trees for fire-fuel and other activities due to growing population. Farming methods are still traditional and farmers strive hard to maximize yield to sustain their families by extending cultivation to the marginal areas and/or lands under mosaic vegetation. As a result, the class rain-fed cropland has shown the highest gain of 1500 ha of land, with an increment rate of 72 ha per year. Population of the area is agrarian, yet firewood is their main source of energy. The border war with Ethiopia has also resulted in massive cutting of wet and dry trees equally for construction of shelters, trenches and for fire wood supply to the army. Besides these human activities, effects of climate change like erratic rainfall and prolonged droughts might have contributed significantly to deforestation in Eritrea, including Tsmieti catchment. According to the Ministry of Land, Water and Environment (MLWE, 2012), increase in temperature, which leads to a high rate of evaporation of moisture from the soil, is a main contributing factor for deforestation in Eritrea. Consequently, these reasons aggravate the process of land degradation through deforestation and accelerated soil erosion.

Barren/degraded land has been also shown a positive increase, where the proportion is almost doubled in the meantime. The proportion of this class in the initial classification is 4.4% or 296 ha, but later it increased to 5.6% (381 ha) and 8.8% (593 ha) in 2002 and 2015, respectively. The statistical analysis shows that the degraded land has expanded by 100% between 1994 and 2015 (Figure 6). Annually 14 ha of land have been converted to degraded barren land. This might be associated mainly with expansion of agriculture practices that result in clearing of shrubs and trees and encourage soil loss through tillage of shallow soils, particularly on slope sides. Conversion of more grazing land into farmlands and other land use types may also result in overgrazing of the already squeezed grazing lands, which can lead to additional degradation of the land.

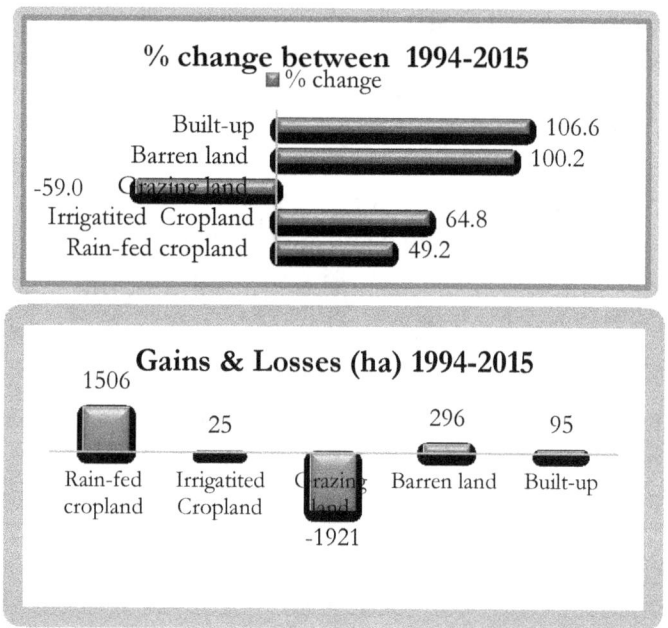

Figure 16. Magnitude and nature of LULC change of the study area, 1994-2015.

A. Change matrix of land use/land cover classes

The change matrix (cross matrix), which shows LULC change between 1994 and 2015, indicates the amount of land (in hectares) from each LULC class that has undergone transformation from one type to another or loss in their areal extents or remained unchanged. The following important points are indicative to understand and analyze the change matrix.

(a) Change matrix is computed for two classifications, where the reference (initial one) is given on top of the column and the classified one (recent year) is along the rows.

(b) Values in each column represent LULC units from the initial classification classes (previous year)

(c) Values in each row give LULC types of the final classification classes (the recent year).

(d) The diagonal values represent units of land, where no change has occurred in a class.

(e) Area measurement is in hectares.

The table was computed by SCP tool and shows the losses and gains of unit of land among the LULC classes. For instance, rain-fed cropland has expanded its areal coverage from 3056 ha in 1994 to 4562 ha in 2015, by taking 1928 ha from grazing land, gained another 141 ha of poor quality barren lands and some small units of land from the rest classes. Inversely, the proportion of grazing land is reduced from 3255 ha in 1994 to 1334 ha in 2015, as a result of its conversion to other classes; 1928 ha to rain-fed cropland, 17 ha to irrigated land, 282 ha to barren lands and 79 ha to built-up area (Table 5). Similarly, the degraded barren lands, gained 210 ha and 282 ha of exhausted lands from rain-fed cropland and grazing land respectively and small units of land from the rest classes to reach 593 ha in the LULC map of 2015. Only the bolded diagonal values represent the class values that remained unchanged, while the rest has undergone changes to some other class type.

The rest of the classes are interpreted in the same way and they deliver similar information. The change matrix indicates the conversion of certain amount of land from built-up area to rain-fed cropland or other LULC classes. However, in reality we don't see that built-up area transformed to agricultural lands. This is most likely associated with the nature of the settlements, being typically scattered and unplanned rural settlement. The available vacant area between individual buildings is used for different purposes, mainly for farm activity and/or planting trees.

	Initial LULC classification of image 1994					
Classes	Rain-fed Cropland	Irrigated Cropland	Grazing land	Barren land	Built-Up	Total
Rain-fed Cropland	**2467**	7	1928	141	19	4562
Irrigated land	20	**22**	17	2	2	63
Grazing land	302	6	**949**	63	14	1334
Barren land	210	1	282	**83**	16	593
Built-Up	57	2	79	7	**38**	183
Total	3056	38	3255	296	89	**6735**

Table 16. Change matrix for the 1994 and 2015 LULC change.

B. NDVI image comparisons

NDVI image comparison provides an important means of assessment of land cover degradation (deforestation) in the area. NDVI score ranges between -1 to 1, where -1 indicates no presence of vegetation, and 1 indicate dense and healthy vegetation. As it can be seen in the maps below (Figure 7), high

NDVI values are shown in areas where there is good vegetation cover. Whereas, non-vegetated areas, including bare soil, river beds, most constructed features have much lower NDVI value. Accordingly, the NDVI results indicate significant change in the land cover of the study area between the two dates of imaging. Land cover of Tsmieti catchment is significantly reduced in the second image of 2015, where an extensive area becomes naked and vulnerable to severe degradation. Nonetheless, the same image of 2015 has also got the highest maximum NDVI value. This is attributed to the presence of irrigated plantations that have perennial plants. These plantation areas appear as clusters of bright green, hence they tend to have highest NDVI value.

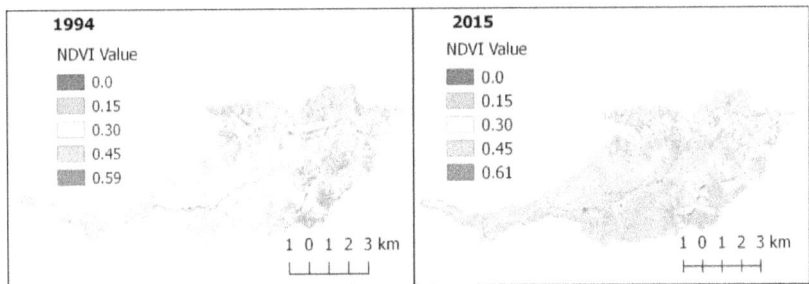

Figure 17. NDVI Image comparisons for Landsat data taken at November 1994 and November 2015.

In addition, the NDVI statistical values given in (Table 6) indicate a marked contrast in land cover change of the area. Such disparity is clearly shown in the mean of the two dates, where the mean of the NDVI image 2015 decreases in certain amount as compared to NDVI mean of 1994.

Statistics	1994	2015
Minimum	-0.78	-0.98
Maximum	0.76	0.82
Mean	0.33	0.28
Standard deviation	0.08	0.09

Table 17. NDVI statistical values.

4. Conclusion

Land degradation is a critical issue in Eritrea, particularly in the highlands region of the country, where Ne'us Zoba Adi Kuala is found. It has severely affected many areas and hence affects people's livelihood negatively. Since land degradation is a process, identifying the geographic area affected by it and assessing its severity however, requires time-series data rather than static data sets as specified by ELD & UNEP (2015). The methodology utilized in the study was compatible to the suggested framework, but challenges remain. These include lack of ample data, and a lack of simplicity for users.

The study, land degradation assessment through LULC change detection, revealed that Tsmieti catchment had been vulnerable to high degree of land degradation. According to the findings, there has been considerable change in LULC pattern of the studied area between 1994 and 2015. LULC change can serve as pointers to the existence or (absence) of land degradation. Especially changes towards cultivable land and bare lands usually make the area more vulnerable to land degradation. Similarly, extensive vegetation cover of Tsmieti catchment has been cleared and deforested for different purposes, including expansion of agriculture practices, settlement and/or exhaust to degraded lands. Currently, there is little or no area left where agriculture could expand, due to high population pressure. Moreover, the areas with some land cover (scant tree cover, shrubs and/or grasses) are used for grazing purposes, which in turn can lead to further land degradation by overgrazing.

The quantitative value of the LULC classes and comparison of the NDVI images over the subsequent periods are evident for the decline in land cover of the area that may well indicate increased land degradation in the study area. The areal proportion of the degraded lands in LULC map of 1994 was 4.4% and the figure rose to 8.8% in the recent map of 2015. Contrary to this, grazing lands, which includes area of open tree cover, shrubs and grasses, have declined from 48% to 20% in the same time. However, land degradation is complex in nature and it is difficult to assess all of its forms in a given area using specific tools and methodology. Therefore, it has to be noted that the proportion of degraded lands on the ground could be significantly higher than the results shown in this study. This is because, some lands classified under croplands or grazing lands could be partially affected by other forms of land degradation like nutrient depletion, compaction, crystallization etc. Many studies have shown that nutrient depletion or exhaustion of organic matter is a type of degradation common in areas where land is used for intensive subsistence farming continuously. Likewise, population size is very large in the area and land has been intensively farmed for centuries with minimal conservation measures. These are surrounded by socio economic and political conditions that encourage land users to overgraze, over cultivate, deforest or pollute their lands.

The results of this specific study have shown the power of remote sensing and GIS in conducting LULC change studies. Satellite data have become valuable tools in studying spatial extent of degraded lands and for monitoring the changes over a period of time. Accordingly, GIS as a tool, specifically the open sources of QGIS, provides a great advantage to analyze multi-temporal remote sensing data. It enables the identification and quantification of areas vulnerable to land degradation in the form land cover change (deforestation). Open source GIS software (QGIS) is a new methodological approach in LULC change research in Eritrea. Thus, GIS not only provides accurate results but is also cost and time-effective way of analysis. Finally, the study suggests that, the methodology used can be applied for regular assessment, monitoring and mapping of widespread land degradation in the country. This can further support conservation planning for sustainable use of environmental resource.

References

African Monitoring of the Environment for Sustainable Development (AMESD) (2011). Land degradation assessment using GIS and Earth Observation for IGAD region (AMESD IGAD Land Degradation Index Bulletin N°. 1)

Araya, Y. H., & Cabral, P. (2010). Analysis and modeling of urban land cover change in Setùbal and Sesimbra, Portugal. *Remote Sensing*, *2*(6), 1549-1563.

Araya, Y. H., & Hergarten, C. (2008). A comparison of pixel and object-based land cover classification: A case study of the Asmara Region, Eritrea. *WIT Transactions on the Built Environment, Geo-Environment and Landscape Evolution III*, *100*, 233-243.

Bai, Z. G., Dent, D., Olsson, L., & Schaepman, M. E. (2008). *Global assessment of land degradation and improvement 1: identification by remote sensing.* Report 2008/01, ISRIC – World Soil Information, Wageningen.

Campbell, J. B., & Wynne, R. H. (2011). *Introduction to remote sensing* (5th ed.). New York: The Guilford Press.

ELD Initiative & UNEP (2015). The economics of land degradation in Africa: Benefits of action outweigh the costs.

Eswaran, H., Lal, R., & Reich, P. F. (2001). Land degradation an overview: Response to land degradation. *Proceedings of the 2nd International Conference on Land Degradation and Desertification*, KhonKaen, Thailand. New Delhi, India: Oxford Press.

FAO (2005). FAO/WFP crop and food supply assessment mission to Eritrea: special report, FAO global information and early warning system on food and agriculture, Rome.

Gashaw, T., Bantider, A., & Mahari, A. (2014). Evaluation of land use/land cover changes and land degradation in Dera Distrit, Ethiopia: GIS and remote sensing based analysis. *International Journal of Scientific Research in Environmental Sciences*, *2*(6), 199-208.

Lillesand, T. M., Kiefer, R. W. & Jonathan, C. (2015). *Remote sensing and image interpretation* (7th ed.). Hoboken, N.J.: John Wiley & Sons, Inc.,

Maitima, J. M., Mugatha, S., Robin, R. S., Gachimbi, L. N., Majule, A., Lyaruu, H., Pomery, D., Mathai, S., & Mugisha, S. (2009). The linkages between land use change, land degradation and biodiversity across East Africa. *African Journal of Environmental Science and Technology, 3*(10), 310-325.

Ministry of Agriculture (MoA), State of Eritrea, Ne'us Zoba Adi Kuala (2016). Unpublished office report, Asmara, Eritrea,

Ministry of Land, Water and Environment (MoLWE), State of Eritrea (2012). Eritrea's Five Years Action Plan (2011-2015) for The Great Green Wall Initiative (GGWI) Draft, Asmara, Eritrea.

MoA (2002). The National Action Program for Eritrea to Combat Desertification and Mitigate the Effects of Drought (NAP). Unpublished office report, Asmara, Eritrea.

Stellmes, M., Sonnenschein, R., Röder, A., Udelhoven T., Sommer, S., & Hill. J. (2015). Land degradation assessment and monitoring of dry lands. In Thenkabail, P. S. (Ed.), *Remote sensing handbook, Vol. III, Remote sensing of water resources, disasters, and urban studies* (pp. 417-451). Boca Raton, FL: CRC Press.

Tewolde, M. G. & Cabral, P. (2011). Urban sprawl analysis and modeling in Asmara, Eritrea. *Remote Sensing, 3*(10), 2148-2165.

Woldetinsae, T., Ogbaghebriel, B., Berhane, K. & Zemenfes, T. (2005). The lands of Eritrea: Their uses and misuses. Unpublished material, University of Asmara, Asmara.

Yengoh, G. T., Dent, D., Olsson, L., Tengberg, A. E., & Tucer, C. J. (2015). *Use of the Normalized Difference Vegetation Index (NDVI) to assess land degradation at multiple scales; Current status, future trends and practical considerations* (1st ed.). Heidelberg: Springer.

Yimer, Zelalem (2015). Land degradation and land management practices in Wollega Zone, Oromia Region. M.Sc. thesis, Haramaya University, Haramaya, Ethiopia.

Land Use-Land Cover Change Detection Using Remote Sensing Data and Geographical Information System (GIS) Tools in Arid Lowlands of Eritrea

Mohammed Mohammedali Mussa[1] Woldeselassie Ogbazghi[2]

Abstract

Over the past five decades, Eritrea has faced serious environmental degradation. To rehabilitate the degraded lands, adaptation and mitigation activities are carried out in the various parts of the country. Despite these activities, Eritrea still lacks a comprehensive Land use and Land cover (LULC) maps; and consequently it is difficult to quantitatively monitor and detect human-induced and natural environmental degradation of a given area over specified period of time. LULC maps are critical tools to monitor and detect environmental changes over time and space. The use of satellite remote sensing and Geographic Information System (GIS) is an effective tool to detect and monitor Land use/Land cover (LULC) changes, mapped and analyzed in a timely and cost-effective manner. The objective of this research was to identify change on LULC between the years 1987 and 2015 using remote sensing and GIS techniques in Hamelmalo sub-Zone, Eritrea. In this study, the area was classified with the help of supervised classification technique and minimum distance algorithm in five main categories: (i) forest and woodland, (ii) shrub/bush land, (iii) Crop land, bare land, (iv) built up and (v) wet land and water bodies. Post-classification comparison change detection algorithm was used to determine changes in LULC in four intervals: 1987-1994, 1994-2002, 2002-2015 and 1987-2015. The result showed that between 1987 and 2015, there was an increase in total area of forest and woodland (3.19%), shrub/bush land (1.49%), Crop land (18.96%) and built up (2.43%). During the same period, bare and wet lands, and water bodies decreased by 25.37% and 1.04% respectively. The study concludes that

---

[1] Lecturer, Department of Land Resources and Environment, Hamelmalo Agricultural College. Email: hameday08@gmail.com.
[2] Associate Professor, Department of Land Resources and Environment, Hamelmalo Agricultural College. Email: wogbazghi@gmail.com.

the level of accuracy of the use of remote sensing data and GIS tools was very high; and the same method can be used to up-scale to map out LULC changes over a larger area of Eritrea to monitor and detect environmental degradation.

Keywords: Land use; land cover; change detection; minimum distance algorithm.

1. Introduction

Eritrea has been vulnerable to climate change with tremendous impact on biodiversity and loss of resilience of the ecosystem (DoE, 2015). Climatic variability and land degradation induce loss of vegetation cover; in which deforestation, overgrazing, and soil erosion being the most evident phenomena in the country (Atsbha *et al.* 1998; Ghebrezgabher *et. al*, 2016; Measho *et al.*, 2019). Hutchinson *et al.* (1991) and Howell & Allan (1990) indicated that the recurrence of drought in the Sahel was a cyclic phenomen affecting the livelihhods' of populations in the drylands. The occurrences of dry spells during the rainy seasons, seasonal droughts and multi-year droughts are nowadays more frequent than ever (DoE, 2015). Since the 1970's the frequency of drought has increased, although without causing famine. During the span of 20 years (1970-1989) Hagos (1995), ERA (1989), Woldeselassie (2018), documented 12 dry years. These droughts were essentially caused by failure of summer (monsoon rains and to some extent the winter, summer or both the winter and summer rains which results in crops failure and massive death of livestock. It also affects the natural vegetation cover and triggers land use changes. Indeed, the vegetation in the highlands and eastern escarpment (1000-1600 m) is shrinking and gradually being replaced by xeric vegetation types. Effects of global climate change and climate variability at the local level has negative impact on the forest cover which is manifested by unpredictable onset and cessation of rainfall, uneven distribution of rain fall spatially and temporally and prolonged droughts (Woldeselassie, 2018). According to Hessel *et al.* (2009); Bobée *et al.* (2012); Brandt *et al.* (2014) and de Waal (1991), climatic anomalies have been documented for the following years: 1960s, 1970s, 1980s, and early 1990s. It is widely accepted that these climate aberrations have significantly contributed to the loss of forest cover in the Sahel region in general and Eritrea.

Land use and land cover change (LULCC) has become a central component in current strategies for managing natural resources and monitoring environmental changes. LULCC caused by human activities is the most important component of global environmental change with impacts possibly greater than the other global changes (Turner *et al.*, 1994 and Jensen, 2005). Humans have been altering land cover since pre-history through the clearance of patches of land for agriculture and livestock (de Sherbinin, 2002). During the past two centuries, the impact of human activities on the land has grown enormously, altering entire landscapes, ultimately impacting on the earth's nature. The results of the pressure include intensified agriculture, decreasing forest cover, loss of biodiversity, land degradation and soil erosion (Pellikka *et al.*, 2004).

In Eritrea, loss of vegetation cover is one of the most significant factors accelerating environmental degradation. This is mainly the consequence of human activities and natural calamities such as drought (climate change) (Atsbha *et al.*, 1998; Nyssen *et al.*, 2004; Ghebrezgabher *et al.*, 2014). Subsistence cultivation and overgrazing exert tremendous pressures on natural resources at large and the forests in particular. The dependence on biomass fuels for domestic household energy remains one of the factors accelerating land degradation. The Eritrean war for independence that lasted for 30 years (1961-1991) is another factor that had altered the vegetation cover forever. Furthermore, unsustainable timber production for the construction of traditional houses adds up to the already precarious condition accelerating deforestation (GoE, 1996).

The Ministries of Land, Water and Environment, and Agriculture indicate that (MoA, 2016), various climate change adaptation and mitigation measures including soil and water conservations, afforestation, reforestation and area closure for natural regenerations were practiced throughout the country. Nevertheless, these activities require continuous monitoring and examination and scrutiny to evaluate their effectiveness, efficiency and sustainability. Research using time series data is also required to quantify the outcomes of such interventions.

To get an up-to-date monitoring of land use and land cover changes, the use of remote sensing and geographic information systems (GIS) technology is increasing worldwide for the identification of patterns in spatial data and vegetation dynamics based on the time-series of satellite imageries (Anderson *et al.*, 2010; Xie *et al.* 2015).

The objective of this study was to detect the changes over the past 30 years through mapping and characterizing the past and present conditions and extent of LU/LC in Hamelmalo sub-Zone of Eritrea using temporal Landsat Thematic Mapper (TM), Enhanced Thematic Mapper (ETM+) and Operational Land Imager (OLI) of 1987, 1994, 2002 and 2015.

2. Methodology

A. Study area

The study was carried out in Hamelmalo sub-Zone, Anseba region of Eritrea located between 15^0 47'34" to 16^0 1'42"N latitude and 38^0 15'32" to 38^0 36'45" E longitude. The study areas exhibit a wide altitudinal differences ranging from arid lowlands to moist highlands. The climate is a semi-arid climate with an average annual temperature of 28°C and average annual rain fall of about 450mm the highest being from June to September. The area is dissected by small streams flowing from the eastern and western mountains and drains into the Anseba River. The Anseba River, which originates from the highlands of Eritrea, bisects the Hamelmalo plains and drains North Westward to Sudan, crossing Habero and Sele'a sub-Zones. The elevation of the study area ranges from 1,154 m on the Hamelmalo plains to 2,167 m above sea level in the peaks of Agombosa mountains in the north east and in Lalmba in the in the west. The total area is 46,867 ha accounting for 7.2% of the total area of Anseba Zone (region).

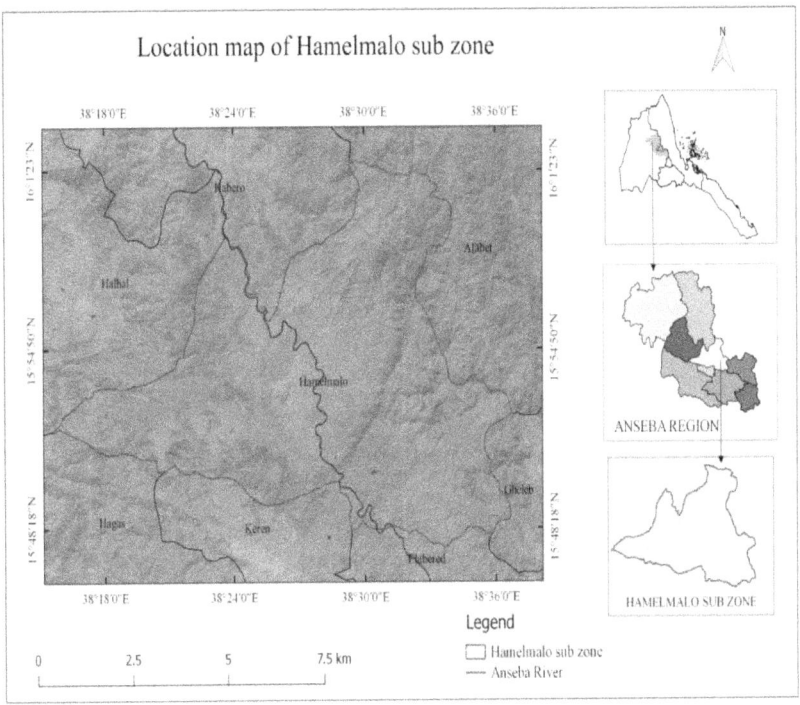

Figure 18. Location of Hamelmalo sub-Zone.

B. Data source

i. Remote sensing data

Three types of satellite images namely (i) Landsat 5 of 1987 and 1994, (ii) Landsat 7 of 2002, and (iii) Landsat 8 of 2015 with 30 mts. spatial resolutions were used. Two satellite image scenes with path 169, row 49 and path 170, row 49 for each of the images of 1994, 2002 and 2015, whereas only one scene (path 170, row 49) for the image of 1987 were used. For modeling sun illumination for topographic correction, Shuttle Radar Topographic Mission (SRTM) digital elevation data with the same resolution to that of the land sat images was used. High resolution SPOT 5 image with spatial resolution of 2.3 m for the image of 2002 and Google Earth maps for images of 1987 and 1994 were also employed to identify different surface features for supporting image classification. The Landsat images for the four different years were analyzed with latest open source software such as Quantum GIS (QGIS), Geographical Resources Analysis Support System (GRASS) and System for Automated Geoscientific Analyses (SAGA). ERDAS EMAGINE 9.1 was also used for mosaicking images.

ii. Field data

Ground reference data were collected using GPS (Garmin) for each Land Use Land Cover Change (LULC) class for LULC training and validation of image classification in which total of 55 representative points were collected from the field in combination with 200 randomly generated points for areas which were not accessible. From these points, 70% were used for training data set and the remaining 30% for validation of image classification for the most recent image of the 2015.

C. Image preprocessing

Topographic correction was applied to mitigate variations in sun illumination using shuttle radar topographic mission (SRTM) for the four different year's satellite images. C-factor method which is mostly used topographic correction method in remote sensing was performed for the correction of the topography. This method was done based on sun azimuth and zenith angles taken from the land sat Metadata.

D. Image classification

In this study, supervised classification method (SCM) with Minimum Distance algorithm was applied for each of the processed satellite images (1987, 1994, 2002 and 2015) to classify the whole study area into six major LULC classes i.e. Forest and woodland, shrub/bush land, crop land, bare land, built up and, wet land and water bodies. Training points collected from the field using GPS for training and validation of image classification were used as inputs.

E. Change detection

Post classification comparison method was used for the change detection of four temporal periods, i.e. 1987-1994, 1994-2002, 2002-2015 and 1987-2015 in SAGA software using cross tabulation and cross classification image.

Figure 19. Conceptual framework used for image processing in sub-Zone Hamelmalo.

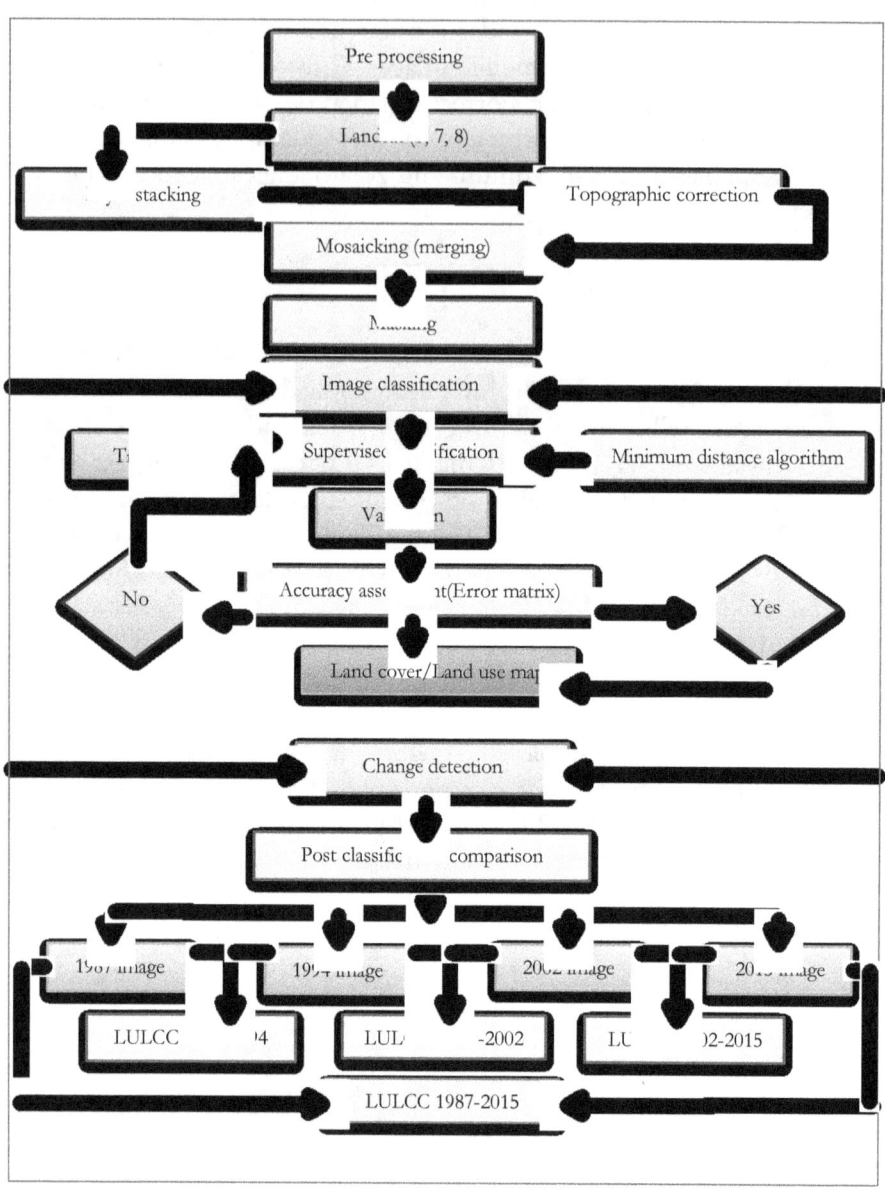

3. Results and Discussions

The study area was classified in to six main classes by the use of supervised technique of classification and minimum distance algorithm and the individual class area and percentage for each year is summarized in Table 1. Thus, land use/land cover maps were generated for four years: 1987, 1994, 2002 and 2015 (Figure 3). The maps depicted that most of the forest and wood land are found in the plane areas especially around the banks of Anseba River with extension towards the western and eastern side of the sub- zone. On the other hand, shrub/bush lands mostly dominate in the western side of the sub -zone to some extent in the east which is located in the mountainous area. In 2015, crop land, in the past, predominately in the central part of the sub-Zone expanded towards the steep slopes.

Land cover/ Land use classes	Area							
	1987		1994		2002		2015	
	(Km²)	(%)	(Km²)	(%)	(Km²)	(%)	(Km²)	(%)
Forest and Wood land	73.9	15.85	102.2	21.82	99.6	21.26	89.2	19.04
Shrub/ bush land	23.5	5.04	46.9	10.01	46.7	9.97	30.6	6.53
Crop land	119.5	25.64	130.2	27.80	162.4	34.66	208.9	44.60
Bare land	241.7	51.86	178.5	38.12	144.8	30.91	124.1	26.49
Built up	0.5	0.11	2.6	0.56	7.6	1.62	11.9	2.54
Wet land and Water bodies	7	1.50	7.9	1.69	7.4	1.58	3.7	0.79
Total	466.1	100	468.3	100	468.5	100.0	468.4	100

Table 18. Summary of each LULC change in area (km²) and percentage from 1987 to 2015.

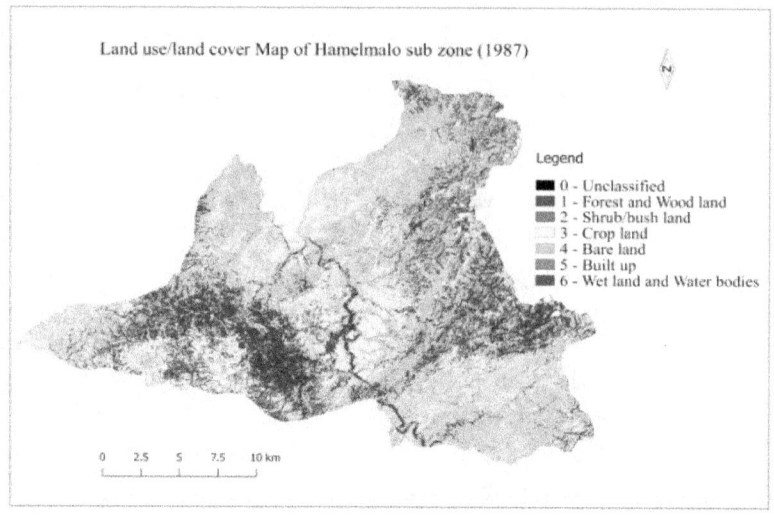

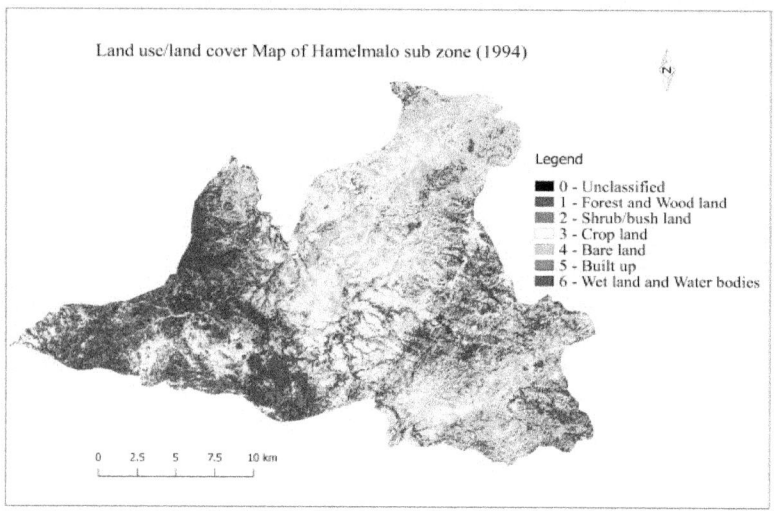

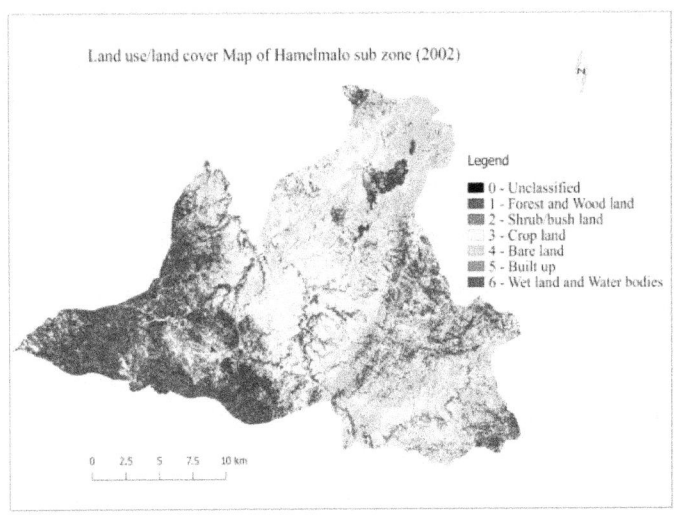

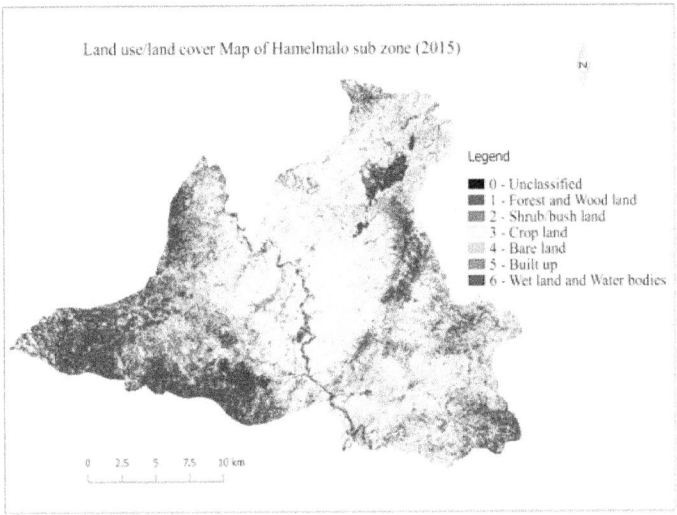

Figure 20. LULC map of Hamelmalo sub-Zone (1987- 2015).

A. Classification accuracy assessment

The results revealed that the overall accuracy for the classified images of 1987, 1994, 2002 and 2015 were 83.3%, 84.4%, 86.8% and 88.4%, with Kappa statistics of 0.77, 0.79, 0.82 and 0.83, respectively (Table 2). According to the explanation and interpretation of kappa statistics, the overall kappa value ranged within substantial agreement for the classified images of 1987 and 1994, and almost perfect agreement for 2002 and 2015. The K_{hat} Coefficient (K) or Kappa statistic measures the difference between the true agreement of classified map and chance agreement of random classifier compared to reference data (Lillesand *et al.*, 2004). Kappa coefficient was calculated using the following formula given by Congalton (1991).

$$K = N \sum_{i=1}^{r} X_{ii} - \sum_{i=1}^{r} (X_{i+} * X_{+i}) / N^2 - \sum_{i=1}^{r} (X_{i+} * X_{+i})$$

where:

K= kappa coefficient
r = the number of rows in the error matrix
X_{ii} = the number of observations in row i column i (along the diagonal)
X_{i+} = is the marginal total of row i (right of the matrix)
X_{+i} = the marginal total of column i (bottom of the matrix)
N = the total number of observations included in the matrix

LULC class	1987		1994		2002		2015	
	prod	use	prod	use	prod	use	prod	use
Forest and wood land	100	91.7	100	87.5	83.3	55.6	100	66.7
Shrub/bush land	100	83.3	100	100	100	100	85.2	100
Crop land,	71.4	50	91.7	68.8	88.9	94.1	95.2	95.2
Bare land	73.9	94.4	66.7	92.3	81	94.4	66.7	100
Built up	100	100	100	100	100	66.7	75	75
Wet land and water bodies	100	100	100	100	100	100	100	50
Overall accuracy	83.3		84.4		86.8		88.4	
Kappa value	0.77		0.79		0.82		0.83	

Table 19. Summary of image classification accuracies (%) for 1987, 1994, 2002 and 2015.
LULC= Land Use Land Cover; PROD=Producer's; USE=User's.

According to Jensen (2005), the probability that a reference pixel is correctly classified, is determined by the producer's accuracy. The probability that a classified pixel from the land cover map accurately corresponds with the referenced data is determined by the user's accuracy.

B. Change detection

In the temporal period of 1987 to 2015, the greatest increase in area change was observed in built up (1,139.8 ha) followed by crop land (8,943.2 ha). During the same period, loss was seen in bare land and wetlands and water bodies which were 11761.5 ha and 327.5 ha respectively (Table 3).

Land use/ Land cover	1987 – 1994		1994 – 2002		2002 – 2015		1987 - 2015	
	Area change (ha)	Area change (%)	Area change (ha)	Area change (%)	Area change (ha)	Area change (%)	Area change (ha)	Area change (%)
Forest and Wood land	2827.7	38.3	-258.2	-2.5	-1039.9	-10.4	1529.6	20.7
Shrub/bush land	2348.8	100.2	-20.7	-0.4	-1609.6	-34.4	718.5	30.6
Crop land	1077.5	9.0	3218.1	24.7	4647.6	28.6	8943.2	74.9
Bare land	-6319.7	-26.1	-3377.8	-18.9	-2064	-14.3	-11761.5	-48.7
Built up	205.6	407.1	502.1	196.1	432.1	57.0	1139.8	2257.0
Wet land and Water bodies	93.3	13.4	-49	-6.2	-371.8	-50.1	-327.5	-47.0

Table 20. Summary of LULC changes for the four temporal periods in (ha) and (%).

Negative number indicates area lost for other land uses.

In terms of conversion between classes, the greatest change was seen from bare land to crop land throughout the study period in which 6,306.8 ha, 6,577.5 ha and 7,194.3 ha between years 1987-1994, 1994-2002 and 2002-2015 respectively were changed. Between 1987 and 2015, 11, 466.1 ha of bare land were converted to crop land throughout the study area (Table 4).

	Land Use, Land Cover							
2015 / 1987	1	2	3	4	5	6	Unclassified	Total
1	0	1,045.3	1,210.2	2,483.3	48.8	99.6	6.4	4,893.6
2	878.6	0	491.1	547.7	47.9	4.6	2.5	1,972.4
3	1,701.2	261.3	0	1,833.9	599.7	1.1	3.5	4,400.7
4	3,487.3	1,319.4	11,466.1	0	461.1	101.5	7.5	16,842.9
5	5.9	0.3	22.7	3.4	0	0	0	32.3
6	306.9	51	39.3	137.1	3.3	0	0.5	538.1
Unclassified	43.4	13.6	114.4	75.7	11.7	3.8	0	262.6
Total	6,423.3	2,690.9	13,343.8	5,081.1	1,172.5	210.6	20.4	28,942.6

*Table 21. Cross-tabulation of LULC change between 1987 and 2015 (area in ha).
Key: (1) Forest and Wood land, (2) Shrub/bush land, (3) Crop land, (4) Bare
land, (5) Built up, (6) Wet land and water bodies.*

4. Conclusion

Despite the diversity of data sources, the remote sensing and GIS data processing yielded very good results in the detection of LULC over a span of three decades. The overall findings showed that built up and crop land increased, whereas bare land decreased throughout the study period. Forest and wood land, and shrub/bush land showed increase in the first temporal period but decreased gradually between 1994–2002 and 2002–2015 and the other way round for wet land and water bodies. More deforestation of forest and woodland and shrub/bush land was detected between 2002 and 2015 to expand the land for agricultural and settlement activities. Moreover, the greatest change was seen from bare land to crop land throughout the study period due to increase of population in the sub - zone from 27,060 in 2002 to 36,000 in 2015. Human induced factors and prolonged droughts and war were the main factors for deforestation in the study area before independence. Hence, Land use and Land cover detection including soil and water conservation and afforestation activities could be detected and monitored using remote sensing data. Thus, this study may be used as an input for land management and policy decision making process. It may also provide an opportunity for environmental management and monitoring of deforestation. The results could be used as a starting point for up- scaling to investigate land use changes' detections at the national or global scales.

Acknowledgement

The first author acknowledges the research grant from the Finish–Eritrea project.

References

Anderson, L. O.; Malhi, Y., Aragäo, L. E. O. C., Ladle, R. J., Arai, E., Barbier, N., & Phillips, O. (2010). Remote sensing detection of droughts in Amazonian forest canopies. *New Phytologist*, *187*(3), 733750.

Atsbha, H., Ghebrestatios, I.. Araya, W., Omer, M., Ogbazghi, W., Ghebremariam, T., & and Ghebreselassie, G. (1998). *Rehabilitation of degraded lands, Eritrea* (2nd ed.). Ministry of Agriculture & University of Asmara.

Bobée, C., Ottle, C., Maignan, F., de Noblet-Ducoudré, N., Maugis, P., Lezine, A.-M., & Ndiaye, M. (2012). Analysis of vegetation seasonality in Sahelian environments using MODIS LAI, in association with land cover and rainfall. *Journal of Arid Environments*, *84*, 38-50.

Brandt, M., Romankiewicz, C., Spiekermann, R., Samimi, C. (2014). Environmental change in time series – An interdisciplinary study in the Sahel of Mali and Senegal. *Journal of Arid Environments, 105*, 52-63.

Congalton, R. (1991). A review of assessing the accuracy of classifications of remotely sensed data. *Remote Sensing of Environment, 37*(1), 35-46.

de Sherbinin, A., Kline, K., & Raustiala, K. (2002). Remote sensing data: Valuable support for environmental treaties. *Environment: Science and Policy for Sustainable Development, 44*(1), 20-31.

de Waal, A. (1991). *Evil days: Thirty years of war and famine in Ethiopia, An Africa Watch report.* New York: Human Rights Watch.

Department of the Environment (DoE), Ministry of Land, Water and Environment, State of Eritrea (2015). Eritrea's Intended Nationally Determined Contribution (INDCs) Report. Asmara, Eritrea.

Eritrean REliefe Associaation (ERA) (1989). Eritrea Relief and Rehabilitation. Sahel: Eritrean Peoples Liberation Front-EPLF.

Ghebrezgabher M. G., Yang T., & Yang X, Wang, X., & Khan, M. Extracting and analyzing forest and woodland cover change in Eritrea based on Landsat data using supervised classification. *Egyptian Journal of Remote Sensing and Space Science, 19*(1), 37-47.

Ghebrezgabher M. G., Yang T., & Yang X. (2014). Remote Sensing and GIS analysis of deforestation and desertification in central highland and eastern region of Eritrea (1972-2014). *International Journal of Sciences: Basic and Applied Research,* 18(2): 161-176.

Government of Eitrea (GoE) (1996). *National Environmental Management Plan (NEMP-E).* Eritrean Environment Agency. Asmara.

Hagos, M. (1995). *Eritrea drought/disaster preparedness strategy submitted to the Intergovernmental Authority on drought and*

Development (IGADD). Asmara, Eritrean Relief and Rehabilitation Agency.

Hessel, R., van den Berg, J., Kaboré, O., van Kekem, A., Verzandovoort, S., Dipama, J.-M., & Diallo, B. (2009). Linking participatory and GIS based land use planning methods: a case study from Burkina Faso. *Land Use Policy, 26*(4), 1162-1172.

Howell, P. P., & Allan, J. A. (1990). *The Nile: Resource evaluation, resource management, hydropolitics and legal issues*. Centre of Near and Middle Eastern Studies, School of Oriental and African Studies, University of London: London:

Hutchinson, R. A., Spooner, B. C., & and Walsh, N. (1991). *Fighting for survival: Insecurity, people and the environment in the Horn of Africa*. Gland, Switzerland: IUCN.

Jensen, J. R. (2005). *Introductory digital image processing: A remote sensing perspective* (3rd ed.). New Jersey: Prentice Hall.

Lillesand, T. M., Kiefer, R. W. & Chipman, J. W. (2004). *Remote sensing and image interpretation* (5th ed.). New York: John Wiley & Sons.

Measho, S., Chen, B., Trisurat, Y., Pellikka, P., Guo, L., Arunyawat, S., Tuankrua, V., Ogbazghi, W., & Yemane, T. (2019). Spatio-temporal analysis of vegetation dynamics as a response to climate variability and drought patterns in the semiarid region, Eritrea. *Remote Sensing, 11*(6), 724-747.

Ministry of Agriculture (MoA), State of Eritrea (2002).*The National Action Programme for Eritrea to combat Desertification and Mitigate the Effects of Droughts*. Asmara, Eritrea.

MoA (2016). *Annual report, Department of Planning and Statistics of the Ministry of Agriculture*. Asmara, Eritrea.

Nyssen, J., Poesen, J., Moeyersons, J., Deckers, J., Haile, M., Lang, A. (2004). Human impact on the environment in the Ethiopian and Eritrean highlands - a state of the art. *Earth-Sceince Reviews, 64* (3 & 4), 273-320.

Ogbazghi, W. (2018). Agro-climatic and environmental hazards and mitigation measures for the Northern and Southern Red

Sea Zone Administrations of Eritrea. *Journal of Eritrean Studies*, *8*(2), 86-131.

Pellika P. K. E., Clark B., Hurskainen, P., Keskinen A., Lanne, M., Masalin, K., Nyman-Ghezelbash, P., & Sirviö, T. (2004). Land use change monitoring applying geographic information systems in the Taita Hills, SE-Kenya. *Proceedings of the 5th African Association of Remote Sensing of Environment Conference, 17-22 Oct. 2004, Nairobi, Kenya.*

Turner, B. L., Meyer, W. B., & Skole, D. L. (1994). Global land-use land-cover change–towards an integrated study. *Ambio*, *23*(1), 91-95.

Xie, B., Jia, X., Qin, Z., Shen, J., & Chang, Q. (2015). Vegetation dynamics and climate change on the Loess Plateau, China: 1982–2011. *Reginal Environmental Change*, *16*(6), 1583-1594.

Evaluation of Accessibility to Primary, Middle and Secondary Schools: Case Study of Adi Qeyyih sub-Zone, Eritrea

Tsinat Yemane[1] and Zemenfes Tsighe[2]

Abstract

Decision makers require spatial information to locate public facilities like schools to ensure that the service is provided optimally. In such cases, a robust decision support system is imperative. Geographic Information System (GIS) is quite a useful tool in determining accessibility to public services. This study assesses accessibility to schools in Adi Keyih sub-Zone using GIS. The Government of the State of Eritrea has been working to expand access to education by locating schools in remote areas in line with the Education for All aim. Despite the concerted efforts, however, like in many African countries, universal access to education is not yet fully achieved in Eritrea. This study sought to assess the problems of accessibility to school in Adi Keyih sub-Zone through inventory mapping and spatial analysis methods, using the national standard for walking distance set by the Eritrean Ministry of Education (MoE). According to the MoE, the maximum standards of walking distance for elementary, middle and secondary schools are 3km, 5km and 7km Euclidean distance (areal distance) respectively. Buffer zones were constructed around each school on the basis of these distance bands to assess accessibility. The study reveals that although the distribution of schools follows the distribution of settlements, many villages remain without access to education. The spatial accessibility results reveal that 15.4% of the villages and 1,658 of the school-age populations (6-18 ages) had no access within 3 km of Euclidean distance from primary school; 18.2% of the villages and 1,704 of the school-age populations (6-18 ages) were

---

[1] Lecturer, Department of Geography, College of Business and Social Sciences. E-mail: tsinatyemane@gmail.com.
[2] Director, Bureau of Higher Education Administration and International Linkages, National Higher Education and Research Institute, Eritrea. Email: zemenfest@gmail.com.

located in inaccessible areas within 5 km of Euclidean distance from middle school and 35.6% of all the villages and 6,159 of the school-age populations were found beyond 7 km of Euclidean distance from the closest secondary school. This study includes relevant recommendation. Among other things, the study strongly recommends upgrading the level of some schools to secondary level and the application of GIS to improve, maintain, and expand access to education.

Keywords: Education; GIS; school catchment area; buffer; accessibility.

1. Background

Education is a fundamental means of development for any nation. Education enables people to improve their lives and change behaviour, as better educated citizens are more productive and contribute better to the development of the country. Proper educational opportunities and the expansion of access to people offer the base for national economic and societal development; they also narrow social inequalities by promoting a meritocratic basis for status attainment (Hannum & Buchmann, 2003). Hence, considering the significance of education for the development of Eritrean societies, culture and economy, the government of Eritrea puts education at center stage in all of its development policies.

Access is one of the major challenges that the Eritrean education system faces; and increasing access to educational opportunity is the overriding policy objectives of the Government of Eritrea (MoE, 2009). Since the liberation of Eritrea in 1991, the Ministry of Education (MoE) has been active in building, renewing, maintaining and equipping schools. However, full access to schooling is not yet achieved and many areas are still educationally uncovered. The Government of the State of Eritrea (GoE) with its development partners is working hard to accomplish the task (MoE, 2003).

The MoE encourages any study that supports the evaluation of accessibility to school centers and that informs decision making in education. In this case, Geographic Information System (GIS) is quite useful. GIS is a computer based system which is being used in the analysis and planning of education. GIS is defined as "... an organized collection of computer hardware, software, geographical data, and personnel designed to efficiently capture, store, update, manipulate, analyse, and display all forms of spatially referenced information" (Heywood, 2011, p. 18). The application of GIS in supporting educational facilities is growing rapidly. Attfield *et al.*, (2001), Al-Rasheed & El-Gamily (2013), Odhiambo & Imwati (2014), Olubadewo *et al.*, (2013) and others have used GIS for supporting educational facilities. Besides, tremendous advancement in GIS tools has enabled researchers to propose efficient methods and approaches to decision makers.

In any area, the maximum usability of any public facility is affected by the level of accessibility. As Ismaila & Yusuf (2006) stated, there are several means of locating public facilities in such a way that the facilities will effectively benefit the majority of people in the society; and one of the techniques employs the accessibility measure. The availability of school center within acceptable distance is of vital importance to attract students and encourage their parents to send them to school. According to the MoE (2009) "due to limited resources and long home-to-school distances, many children in basic education are still withdrawing before mastering the essential basic skills"(p. 6). Therefore, to improve access, it is necessary to investigate and monitor the distribution of school facilities. The GIS technology is quite a powerful tool in determining accessibility.

Few attempts have been made to evaluate the distribution and accessibility of public facilities in Eritrea using GIS. For instance, Measho (2009) made a study on the physical accessibility of places to public health care facilities using GIS. One of Eritrea's

Educational Strategies is to apply GIS for the improvement and expansion of access to schools through school mapping for the effective and efficient use of schools by the target school-age population. However, to the best knowledge of the author, there is no study done so far on educational facilities that applied GIS. Hence, this study embarked on the application of GIS to evaluate accessibility of settlements to schools in Adi QeyyiH sub-Zone. The study makes use of buffer zone analysis to evaluate spatial accessibility of settlements to schools.

2. Statement of problem

In Eritrea, many rural villages are located far away from the nearest school, as in many developing countries. Student need to walk for hours to reach their schools. Students who travel long distance face numerous challenges. To mention a few examples, they become hungry during the early hours of their class; they become physically exhausted, hindering them from following their lessons attentively; and they face difficulty doing their homework. Many families refrain from sending their children, especially girls, to distant schools in fear of the risks that such distances entail. Families fear that young male mates may attack their daughters on the way to home or school; they are also afraid of wild animals when they have to walk during dark hours of the day (Zayd, 2001).

In the area where this research is conducted, many students traverse long distance from their settlement sites to the schools especially those who cannot afford to rent house near the school or buy a bicycle as an alternative solution. This could be one of the reasons for students to quit school. In addition, the spatial distribution of schools in Adi QeyyiH sub-Zone is unequal. It has high concentration of schools in the south-central part, while the northern and north-eastern part of the area has low share of schools. Therefore, people residing in the northern and north-eastern areas have low level of access.

3. Significance of the study

The large number of student dropouts from school tends to suggest that there are certain factors that discourage students from staying in school and completing their studies. Access to school is considered as one of the factors that impede students from completing their studies, especially in remote and scattered settlements. Therefore, studying the impacts of accessibility to school is of vital importance for informed educational decision making. The results of this study are thus expected to:

(a) provide information on the level of accessibility to schools;
(b) demonstrate GIS as an educational decision support tool; and
(c) provide a base line for further research on the problem of accessibility to education.

4. Research objective

The main objective of this study is to analyze accessibility of the current schools in the study area by applying spatial analysis tools in order to identify areas that are not accessible to school by the distance standards of the MoE.

5. Research question

The study attempts to answer the following research question related to the above objective is: are there settlements which are too far (beyond walking standards of MoE) from the location of schools?

6. Study area

This study is conducted at *Ne'us Zoba* (sub-Zone) level. The sub-Zone selected is Adi QeyyiH, which is located in the North-Eastern part of *Zoba Debub* (Southern Administrative Region). It has a total area of approximately 600 km^2 (EMIC, 2015). It is located between latitudes 14° 50' N and 15° 6' N, and longitude 39° 13' E and 39° 31' E. The elevation varies from 1059 mts. to 2862 mts. above mean sea level. As per 2017 data, Adi QeyyiH sub-Zone had 24 schools, including elementary, middle and secondary schools.

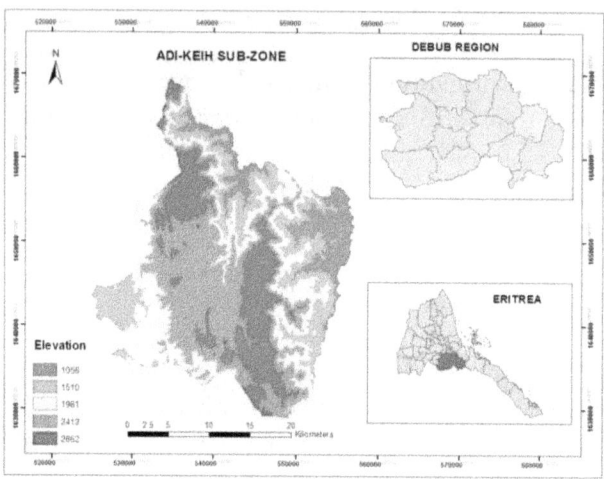

Figure 21. Study area.

7. Concept of accessibility

The concept of accessibility has been used by many researchers in a number of different fields (see, e.g., Makrí & Folkessson, 1999; Ogunyemi *et al.*, 2014; Aliyu *et al.*, 2013; Odhiambo & Imwati, 2014; Olubadewo *et al.*, 2013; Black *et al.*, 2004; Karou & Hull, 2012; Ngigi *et al.*, 2012; Agrawal & Gupta, 2016; Ismaila & Yusuf,

2006; Brabyn & Skelly, 2002; Rodriguez, 2015). Accessibility is a crucial concept for decision making. It evaluates the availability and quality of basic services in an area and reflects the ease of reaching needed or desired activity (Handy and Clifton, 2001). Accessibility to schools is determined by the capability of a person to reach a destination (Rodriguez, 2015). Students who are residents in a place with high access can reach their school with low effort and/or cost (distance, time), while students who reside in a low access places reach their school with high effort and/or cost. Accessibility is not only described by the amount of effort required by a person to reach a destination but it is also described by the number of activities (such as goods and communication) which can be reached from a certain location (Ogunyemi et al., 2014). Rodriguez (2015) explained that location and distances are the two main parameters that are used to describe accessibility. In this study, distance is understood as the separation between schools the students attend and the villages in which they reside. Accessibility is used to support planners and decision makers in locating public facilities where usability is maximized. This is one of the reasons why accessibility has importance in locating and assessing public facilities such as schools. However, locating public facilities in places where the majority of the community can benefit is not an easy task (Ismaila & Yusuf, 2006). Vuri (2007) argues that, in many rural areas of developing countries, difficult access to schools in terms of long distance from nearest school or high travel cost might have a non-negligible effect on why many children do not attend school at all or reason for dropout. While Ismaila & Yusuf (2006) claimed that, better accessibility of public facilities ensures economic efficiency in the use of such facilities because when they serve more people, they would be more cost effective.

Accessibility can be measured using different methods and the different measurements can give different results of the area of interest. Often, there is no single method or unit that conveys all of the information needed for evaluation. It should also be borne in mind that different measurement units represent different perspectives and assumptions. As stated by Makrí & Folkessson (1999) four major types of measurements are typically used for measuring accessibility: "distance measures, cumulative-opportunity measure, gravity-based measure and utility-based measures" (pp. 4-6).

Distance measures, which involve counting the distance from one location to different centers of opportunities, are the simplest measures of accessibility. Distance is often measured as average distance, weighted area distance or distance to the closest opportunity. The estimation of these distances can be performed in several ways; "Euclidean distance, Manhattan distance, Least Cost Path and Shortest network time" (Makrí & Folkessson, 1999, p. 4) are some the distance measures used. This present study uses Euclidean distance to measure accessibility of settlements to school centers using vector buffer analysis.

Gravity-opportunity measure is another type of measurement which is "derived from the denominator of the gravity model used to predict trip distribution; these measures weigh the amount of activity at different destinations by the cost, time, or distance to get there" (Handy & Clifton, 2001, p. 68). It is obtained by weighting opportunities in an area with a measure indicating their attraction and discounting them by impedance measure (Makrí & Folkessson, 1999). A cumulative-opportunities measures "count the number of opportunities reached within a given distance or travel time and gives an indication of the range of choices available to residents" (Handy & Clifton, 2001, p. 68). The last type of measurement is utility-based measurement in which "the probability of an individual making a particular choice depends on the utility of that choice relative to the utility of all choices; the accessibility measure comes from the denominator of the model and reflects the total utility of all choices" (Handy & Clifton, 2001. p. 69).

8. Analytical framework of the study

The analytical framework of the research study is carried out by relating the national walking distance with the concept of accessibility, and evaluates accessibility using buffer zone analysis.
The maximum walking standards for students to get access varies from level to level. According to the Ministry of Education, Research and Human Resource Department (RHRD), the maximum standards of walking distance for basic education should not exceed 3km while the maximum walking distance for middle and secondary level are 5km and 7km respectively. The local areas that have access within the mentioned national distance standards are considered as having high access while areas beyond the maximum national standards are considered as having low access. However, it should be noted that, this national walking distance standards is a working policy only.

9. Methodology

A. Data source and acquisition

The coordinates of all schools and settlements in Adi QeyyiH sub-Zone were obtained from the MoE and Eritrea Mapping and Information Center (EMIC). Besides, these coordinates were checked using GPS (Garmin Oregon 650) during the field visit. The attributes of school data sets comprised of X (easting) and Y (northing) coordinates, school id, school category by level (primary, middle and secondary) whereas the attributes of settlement data sets consisted of several data attributes such as X and Y coordinates, administrative name, village name, village code, population data. In many studies on modelling of physical accessibility, the coordinates of school and settlement locations are used to measure the level of accessibility (e.g., Aliyu *et al.*, 2013; Al-Rasheed & El-Gamily, 2013; Agrawal & Gupta, 2016; Olubadewo *et al.*, 2013; Ogunyemi *et al.*, 2014). This study uses these pair of coordinates wherever necessary in the study.

B. Software

The research study uses QGIS version 2.18 (Quantum GIS) to make spatial analyses of the aforementioned data sets and produce maps. QGIS is open source software which provides simple and powerful tools for analysing and visualising spatial data.

C. Methods

The specific method employed to achieve the objectives of the research is briefly outlined below.

The spatial analysis works of this study begun by extracting the spatial distribution of schools and villages using the common geoprocessing tool – clipping; using the data acquired from MoE and EMIC. To answer the question raised in this study several spatial analyse tools (such as buffer, overlays, point-in-polygon and clipping) available within QGIS were used. As with many other studies, the study applied GIS to examine accessibility of settlements to school centers (see, e.g., Agrawal and Gupta, 2016; Ngigi *et al.*, 2012; Aliyu *et al.*, 2013; Al-Rasheed & El-Gamily, 2013; Odhiambo & Imwati, 2014; Olubadewo *et al.*, 2013; Ogunyemi *et al.*, 2014).

Vector map buffer analysis was undertaken by creating 3km, 5km, and 7 km buffer zones to define the catchment area of primary, middle and secondary schools respectively. Buffer analysis is good enough to determine area of influence of a feature (point, line, or polygon). Accordingly, the level of accessibility in the area is determined by overlaying the point dataset (schools) over the polygon (Adi QeyyiH sub-Zone). The measurement used to determine level of accessibility is Euclidean distance. Euclidean distance cannot be considered as real distance, as it measures the distance as the crow flies (straight line). However, Euclidean distance measurement is more appropriate to find approximate distance measurements than real distance especially in places where clear real routes do not exist, and where people may use different travel routes from the same origin to a given destination. Hence in this study, Euclidean distance measurement is employed to assess accessibility of settlements to schools, and where road distance data is not available (Measho, 2009). Additionally, it is a common distance assumption in many geographic models (Tobler, 1993), and used widely in accessibility studies. For example, Odhiambo & Imwati (2014) applied buffer analysis using Euclidean distance to determine service areas of educational facilities by creating polygons to a specified distance around the facilities.

10. Results and discussions

A. Spatial distribution of schools and settlements

The field survey and data collected revealed that there were 24 schools in Adi QeyyiH sub-Zone in 2017; out of which fourteen (14) were elementary schools, seven (7) were middle school and the remaining three (3) were secondary schools. Almost all of the schools were public (governmental) school; only one school is non-governmental. The sub-Zone is divided into 21 administrative localities, comprising of 106 villages and a total population of 62,027 (administration of Adi QeyyiH sub-Zone, 2017). Figure 2 below show the distributional pattern of schools and settlements in Administrative of Adi QeyyiH sub-Zone.

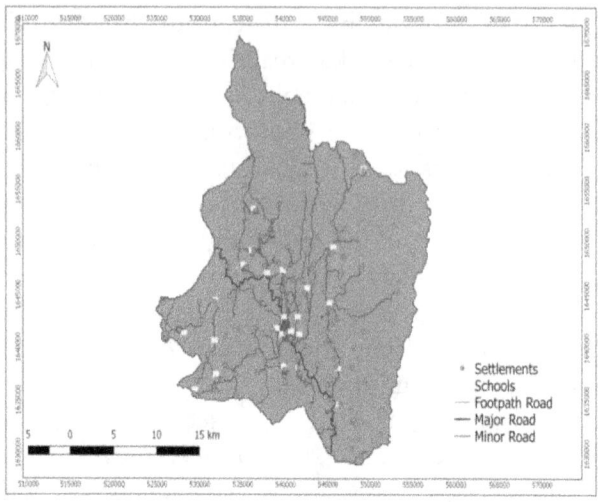

Figure 22. Distribution of schools & settlements.

B. Spatial accessibility to schools

As stated above, the accessibility of settlements to schools is assessed using buffer analysis. The analysis is conducted for primary, middle and secondary schools. Figures 3-5 below depict the catchment areas of primary, middle and secondary schools respectively. To evaluate the level of access, the study used the walking distance standard of MoE for different school levels. As stated above, the walking distance of primary school students should not exceed 3km; that of middle school students 5km and that of secondary school students 7km. Therefore, villages located beyond the specified distance bands for primary, middle and secondary schools are considered as inaccessible.

Figure 3 shows the 3000 mts. buffer zones around the primary schools determining the area coverage of primary schools. Villages enclosed within the specified buffer zones are recognized as accessible while villages outside the specified buffer zones are considered as inaccessible to primary school. According to the figure, most villages have good access to primary schools. A spatial valuation based on access to primary school revealed that 84.6% of the villages are found within the specified buffer zones (3000 m.) of straight line distance while 15.4% of the villages had no primary school within 3000 mts. straight distance. Students who may try to attend school from such distant villages run high risk of dropout, low educational achievement, physical exhaustion, sexual harassment and so on.

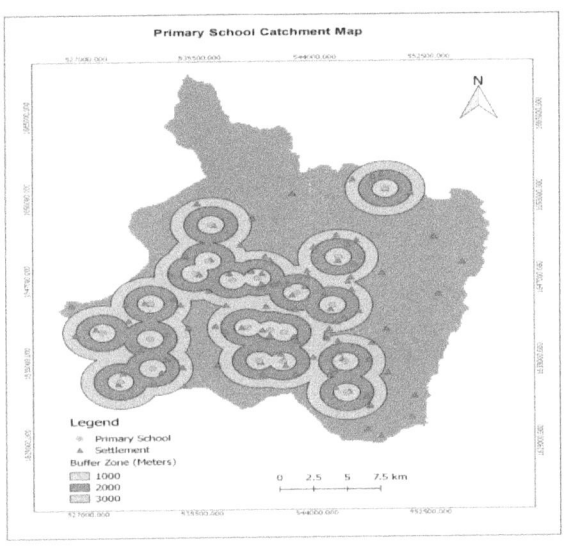

Figure 23. Villages covered by each primary school.

Distance	1000 mts.	2000 mts.	3000 mts.	>3000 mts.
Primary school	30.8%	26%	27.8%	15.4%

Table 22. 3000 mts. buffer zone around primary schools.

Similarly, Figure 4 shows the 5000 mts. buffer zones around middle schools to determine the area coverage of middle schools. The map shows that 81.8% of the villages are found within 5km of straight line distance whereas 18.2% have low access to any middle school.

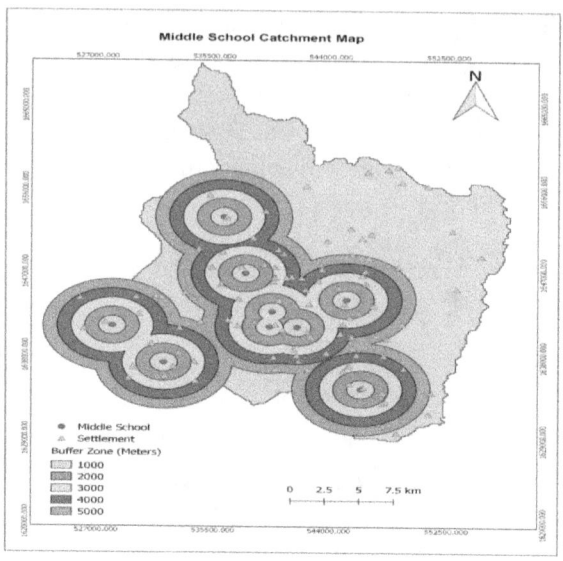

Figure 24. Villages covered by each middle school.

Distance	1000 mts.	2000 mts.	3000 mts.	4000 mts.	5000 mts.	>5000 mts.
Middle school	7.7%	12.5%	23.1%	23.1%	15.4%	18.2%

Table 23. 5000 mts. buffer zone around middle schools.

Figure 5 shows the 7000 mts. buffer zones around the secondary schools to determine coverage areas of secondary schools. Compared to primary and middle schools; many villages have low access to secondary schools. More than one-third of the villages are located beyond the 7km of straight distance from the closest secondary school.

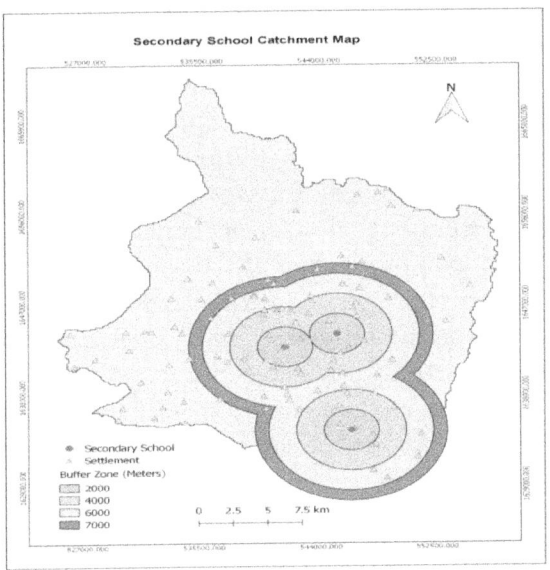

Figure 25. Villages covered by each secondary school.

Distance	2000 mts.	4000 mts.	6000 mts.	7000 mts.	>7000 mts.
Secondary school	9.6%	23.1%	23.1%	8.6%	35.6%

Table 24. 7000 mts. buffer zone around secondary schools.

Using the home-to-school distance of schools defined by MoE, further analysis is undertaken to calculate the spatial coverage of primary, middle and secondary schools separately. The results suggested that out of the total area (600 km²) of Adi QeyyiH sub-Zone, the catchment area for all of the primary schools accounts for 197.4 km², or 32.9% of the total area. The space covered by the catchment area of middle and secondary schools are 141.3 km² (23.6%) and 66 (11%) km² respectively. In general, the results show that larger area had access to primary schools compared to middle and secondary schools. Therefore, taken the 3km straight line distance as a threshold to determine accessibility to primary level education, there were 16 villages (out of 106 villages) having 1,658 school aged population (6-18) living in areas with low accessibility to primary schools; the school aged population living in areas of low accessibility to middle and secondary schools, that is outside the 5 km and 7 km buffers, were 1,704 and 6,159 respectively and the number of villages which had low access to middle and secondary schools accounted for 20 and 38 respectively. The high proportion of access by population and low access by geographic area mirrors the mismatch between population distribution and geographical area. Large portions of the study area are sparsely populated and schools here are few and far apart. Hence large areas are in the sparsely populated northern and north-eastern parts of the study area lie outside the school catchment areas.

In many studies, spatial accessibility of public facilities like schools is assessed using international standards. For example, Ogunyemi et al., (2014) applied UNESCO's walking standards (2km) to evaluate the level of accessibility to secondary schools in Nigeria. However, in this study the national walking distance standard stated by the MoE is used to assess physical accessibility of settlements to primary, middle and secondary schools. It is, thus, obvious that the results of this study are not directly comparable with the results of similar studies done in other countries. Having stated this, the findings of Ogunyemi et al., (2014) revealed that 49.4% of students travelled more than 2km suggesting that these students were disadvantages in terms of distance to school. The finding of present study reveals that 84.6%, 81.8% and 64.4% of the settlements of Adi QeyyiH sub-Zone have access to primary, middle and secondary schools respectively, and suggest that most of the settlements have access (especially to primary and middle schools) within the predefined national standards. It is quite obvious, however, that if the study were to use the UNESCO standard, the proportion of settlements with access to schools would be much lower than the proportions stated above.

In general, settlements have less access to secondary schools, moderate access to middle schools and relatively higher access to primary schools. Thus, if the predefined walking distance from a nearest school center is applied as a vantage point for planning and policy making, there are some villages that may need attention. For instance, in the area where the study is undertaken the level of accessibility to primary school is pretty fair than middle and secondary schools. This means that most of the villages have access to primary school within the predefined walking distance standard of MoE. Relatively, the level of access to middle school is better than access to secondary schools; there are only 3 secondary schools (Igila, Safira and Adi QeyyiH) that offer secondary level education for more than 100 villages in the area.

11. Conclusion

The aim of this study is to evaluate accessibility of schools in Adi QeyyiH sub-Zone using the application of GIS. The method used in this study be used to support educational decision system; and particularly to develop an educational strategy to improve accessibility. Moreover, it could also help to comprehend how access to school influences the service quality of the educational sector.

The Government of the state of Eritrea aims at universal coverage of primary education. The result from spatial assessment of physical accessibility based upon Euclidean distance measurement shows that there was wide coverage of primary education in Adi QeyyiH sub-Zone and thus supports the government's policy. compared to the coverage of elementary education, the coverage area of middle and secondary schools were moderate and low respectively. This implies that certain students who complete primary school may not continue middle school and some of those students who manage to complete their middle school may not pursue secondary school due to long home-to-school distance. Therefore, the transition of students from elementary to secondary school may not be smooth. This in turn may lead to high attrition rates. Such a critical result will enable the decision makers and planners to prioritize the immediate action of relocating schools or widen the accessibility wherever necessary.

The findings of this study could be used by the Ministry of Education explore options to enhance accessibility to schools. For example, as there was inadequate number of secondary schools, the number of schools that provide secondary education could be increased by upgrading the level of some middle schools to secondary level. In addition, in order to increase attendance of students in the schools, the government may establish boarding and para-boarding schools.

Furthermore, the study evidently shows the importance of GIS in supporting educational decision system and specifically to improve access to education in the area using different spatial analysis tools. Thus, the MoE could adopt GIS as educational decision support system for development and expansion of access and equity. Thus, capacity building in GIS through collaborative partnership is necessary.

References

Agrawal, S., & Gupta, R. D. (2016). School mapping and geospatial analysis of the schools in Jasra development block of India. *The International Archives of the Photogrammetry, Remote Sensing and Spatial Information Sciences, Volume XLI-B2, 2016 XXIII ISPRS Congress, 12–19 July 2016, Prague, Czech Republic,* 145-150.

Aliyu, A., Shahidah, M. A., and Aliyu, R. M., (2013). Mapping and spatial distribution of post primary schools in Yola North local government area of Adamawa State, Nigeria *International Journal of Science and Technology*, 2(5), 405-422.

Al-Rasheed, K. and El-Gamily, I. H. (2013). GIS as an efficient tool to manage educational services and infrastructure in Kuwait. *Journal of Geographic Information System*, 5(1), 75-86.

Attfield, I., Tamiru, M., Bruno, P., & de Grauwe, A. (2001). *Improving micro-planning in education through a Geographical Information System Studies on, Ethiopia and Palestine*. International Institute for Educational Planning, Paris: UNESCO.

Black, M., Steeve, E., Patricia, N. A., Manuel, V., and Zine, El. M. (2004). *Using GIS to measure physical accessibility to health care*. https://proceedings.esri.com/library/userconf/health04/papers/pap3023.pdf.

Brabyn, L. and Skelly, C. (2002). Modelling population access to New Zealand public hospitals. *International Journal of Health Geographics*, 1(1), 1-9.

Eritrean Mapping and Information Center (EMIC), Map, 2015.

Handy, S., & Clifton, K. (2001). Evaluating neighbourhood accessibility: Possibilities and practicalities. *Journal of Transportation and Statistics*, 4(2), 67-78.

Hannum, E. & Buchmann, C. (2003). *The consequences of global educational expansion: social science perspectives*. Cambridge, MA: American Academy of Arts and Sciences.

Heywood, I., Cornelius, S., & Carver, S. (2011). *An introduction to geographical information systems* (4th ed.). New Jersey: Prentice Hall.

Ismaila, A. & Yusuf, A. A. (2006). GIS and space syntax: Analysis of accessibility to urban green areas in Doha district of Dammam metropolitan area, Saudi Arabia. *Environment and Ecology*. https://www.researchgate.net/profile/Ismaila-Rimi-Abubakar/publication/256088381_GIS_and_space_syntax_an_an alysis_of_accessibility_to_urban_green_areas_in_Doha_district_of _Dammam_metropolitan_area_Saudi_Arabia/links/546083d30cf2 95b5616202a3/GIS-and-space-syntax-an-analysis-of-accessibility-to-urban-green-areas-in-Doha-district-of-Dammam-metropolitan-area-Saudi-Arabia.pdf.

Karou, S. & Hull, A. (2012) Accessibility measures and instruments. In Hull, A., Silva, C., & Bertolini, L. (Eds.) (pp. 1-19), *Accessibility instruments for planning practice*. COST Office.

Makrí, M.-C., & Folkessson, C. (1999). Accessibility measures for analyses of land use and travelling with Geographical Information Systems. *Proceedings from the Annual Transport Conference at Aalborg University*, 6(1), 1-17.

Measho, S. (2009). Modelling relative physical accessibility of populated places to public health care facilities in Eritrea. M.Sc. thesis, School of Geography, Birkbeck College University of London.

Ministry of Education (MoE) of the State of Eritrea (2003). National education policy. Asmara: Eritrea.

MoE (2009). National education policy. Asmara, Eritrea.

Ngigi, M. M., Douglas, M., & Francis, O. M. (2012). Planning and analysis of educational facilities using GIS. A Case Study of Busia County, Kenya. AGSE 2012–FOSS4G-SEA, 261.

Odhiambo, O. G. & Imwati, A. T. (2014). Use of Geo-Information systems for educational services provision and planning in Asal area, Kenya: *International Journal of Science and Research*, 3(9), 2432-2446.

Ogunyemi, S. A., Muibi, K. H., Ezekiel, E. O., Fabiyi, O. O., & Halilu A. S. (2014). A geospatial approach to evaluation of accessibility to secondary educational institution in Ogun State, Nigeria. IOP Conf. Series: *Earth and Environmental Science*, 20 (2014) 012045.

Olubadewo, O. O., Abdulkarim, I. A., and Ahmed, M. (2013). The use of GIs as educational decision support system for primary schools in Fagge local government area of Kano state, Nigeria. *Academic Research International*, 4(6), 614-624.

Rodríguez, J. (2015). Walkability study for school accessibility: Case study of the San Juan, Puerto Rico Elementary Schools.

M.Sc. thesis, Faculty of the USC Graduate School, University of Southern California.

Tobler, W. (1993). Three presentations on geographical analysis and modelling: Non-isotropic modelling speculations on the geometry of geography global spatial analysis. Technical Report 93-1, University of California, Santa Barbara.

Vuri, D. (2007). The effect of availability and distance from school on children's time allocation in Ghana and Guatemala. Understanding Children's Work Programme Working Paper.

Zayd, Tecle. (2001). An investigation of low participations and dropouts of girls of primary school, Saho ethnic group in sub-Zone, Senafe, Eritrea. Master's thesis, Faculty of NIEPA, New Delhi.

Previous issues of the journal

Journal of Eritrean Studies

| Volume VI | Number 1 | July 2012 |

Contents

ARTICLES

Senai Wolde-Ab
Protection under the scanty law of author's rights (copyright) in Eritrea

Saleh Mahmud Idris
Dahalik: An endangered language or a Tigre variety?

Tesfay Tewolde
Apparent biliteral verbs in Tigrinya

Abbebe Kifleyesus
Children's cultures: Some conceptual issues and research potentials in highland Eritrea

Ghebrehiwet Medhanie
Aloes of Eritrea: The need for their conservation

BOOK REVIEW

Kab Rix' Ḥəfnti (ካብ ሪእ ቐ ሕፍን ቲ) **by Tekie Beyene**
Reviewed by Abraham Tesfalul

JOURNAL OF ERITREAN STUDIES

| Volume VI | Number 2 | December 2012 |

ARTICLES

Charles Cantalupo
Literature, power, translation and Eritrea

Khalid Mohammed Idris
Towards a sustained use of Adhanet improved biomass cook stove: Issues in dissemination

Alessandro Volterra
Recruiting askaris (1885-1896): Military requirements and jurisdiction in Italian official documents and personal memoirs

Zemenfes Tsighe, Stifanos Hailemariam, Senai Woldeab, Goitom Mebrahtu, Selamawi Sium, Meseret Bokuretsion, Hagos Ahmed, Ghidey Gebreyohannes, Andemariam Gebremicael and Giorgio Solomon
Tobacco use and control: A national survey of students in Eritrea

BOOK REVIEWS

Joining Africa: From Anthills to Asmara by Charles Cantalupo,
Tej N. Dhar

Məʿbul Mäzgäbä-Qalat English-Tigrinya (English-Tigrinya dictionary), by Tekie Tesfai
Saleh Mahmud Idris

Research Journal of the College of Arts and Social Sciences   ISSN: 2308-0752

JOURNAL OF ERITREAN STUDIES

| Volume VII | Number 1 | December 2014 |

ARTICLES

Tej N. Dhar
The Novelist v/s the Critic: Beyene Haile and the strange case of *Is He Mad?*

Musa Hussein Naib
The challenges of equitable provision of quality education in Eritrea: A social justice perspective

M. Raouf Hamed, Dawit Tesfai Mehari and Tsehaye Gilai Tesfaldet
Eritrean pharmaceutical achievements during the struggle (1961 – 1991): A portrayal assessment

Berhane Demoz
Educational needs of elementary school students and its implications to initial teacher education programs

BOOK REVIEW

Ascari Tales: A Review of Gebreyesus Hailu's The Conscript
Reviewed by Christine Matzke

The Conscript by Gebreyesus Hailu; Trans. Ghirmai Negash
Reviewed by Tej N. Dhar

Research Journal of the College of Arts and Social Sciences   ISSN: 2308-0752

JOURNAL OF ERITREAN STUDIES

| Volume VII | Number 2 | June 2016 |

Health and Society: The Biology of Disease and Anthropology of Illness in Eritrean Studies

Special Issue Editor
Abbebe Kifleyesus

Abbebe Kifleyesus
Introduction: Epistemology of the Biology of Disease and Anthropology of Illness

ARTICLES

Abbebe Kifleyesus
'Nobody Will Marry Somebody with Children Already': The Cultural Construction of HIV/AIDS Transmission and Condom Utilisation in a Nascent Nation

Abraham Zerai
Mental Illness in a Cultural Sense in Asmara and its Surroundings

Abrehet Gebrekidan
Reintegration of Obstetric Fistulae Survivors in Eritrea

Eyoab Iyasu and **Muntaser E. Ibrahim**
Genetic Analysis of Extant Eritrean Populations and its Relevance to Genomics and Health

Tekeste Fekadu
Envenoming Snakebites in Eritrea: A Preliminary Study

Abbebe Kifleyesus
IM MEMORIUM: Brother Ezio Tonini (1939-2016)

Research Journal of the College of Arts and Social Sciences   ISSN: 2308-0752

JOURNAL OF ERITREAN STUDIES

| Volume VIII | Number 1 | September 2017 |

ARTICLES

Ghiorgis Tekle and Hagos Fesshaye
An Assessment of Factors that Influence Youth Entrepreneurship in the Context of Eritrea

Khalid Mohammed Idris, Yonas Mesfun Asfaha and Mohammed Ali Ibrahim
Teachers' Voices, Challenging Teaching Contexts and Implications for Developing Teacher Education in Eritrea

Ageeb Elamin
Deviant Pronunciation Forms Produced by College Tigrinya-speaking Learners of English

BOOK REVIEWS

ኤርትራ፡ ካብ ፈደረሽን ናብ ጐበጣን ሰውራን 1956-1962 (Eritrea: From Federation to Annexation and Revolution 1956-1962) by Alemseged Tesfai
Reviewed by Salahadin Ali

The Askaris, From the Roots of a Nation to its Fruition. An Assessment of the Documentary History of the Askaris (1931-1941), by **Alessandro Volterra**
Reviewed by Kiflom Michael

A Thematic Introduction to Human Geography, by Woldetinsae Tewolde
Reviewed by Khalid Mohammed Idris

Research Journal of the College of Arts and Social Sciences   ISSN: 2308-0752

JOURNAL OF ERITREAN STUDIES

| Volume VIII | Number 2 | December 2018 |

Assessment of Hazards and Community-based Mitigation Measures for the Northern and Southern Red Sea Zone Administrations of Eritrea

Special Issue Guest Editors
Ghebrebrhan Ogubazghi and Zemenfes Tsighe

Ghebrebrhan Ogubazghi and Zemenfes Tsighe
Introduction to the Special Issue

ARTICLES

Zemenfes Tsighe
Hazards: Conceptual Frameworks and Mitigation Approaches in the Context of Northern and Southern Red Sea Zone Administrations of Eritrea

Woldeselassie Ogbazghi, Zekeria Abdelkerim, Woldetensae Tewolde, and Ghebrebrhan Ogubazghi
Agro-ecological and Livelihoods Profiles of the Northern and Southern Red Sea Zone Administrations of Eritrea

Woldeselassie Ogbazghi
Agro-climatic and Environmental Hazards and Mitigation Measures for the Northern and Southern Red Sea Zone Administrations of Eritrea

Zekeria Abdelkerim
Coastal and Marine Disasters in the Eritrean Coast of the Red Sea and their Mitigation Measures

Ghebrebrhan Ogubazghi and Andemichael Solomon
Geohazards and Mitigation Measures for the Northern and Southern Red Sea Zone Administrations of Eritrea

Woldetensae Tewolde
Community-based Disaster Risk Reduction Measures in the Northern and Southern Red Sea Zone Administrations of Eritrea

Melake Tewolde
Disaster Risk Management and Economic Development Options for the Northern and Southern Red Sea Zone Administrations of Eritrea

Research Journal of the College of Arts and Social Sciences   ISSN: 2308-0752

www.ingramcontent.com/pod-product-compliance
Lightning Source LLC
Chambersburg PA
CBHW070951120726
47910CB00004B/1199